WORCESTERSHIRE
PLACE-NAMES

ANTHONY POULTON-SMITH

SUTTON PUBLISHING

First published in 2003 by
Sutton Publishing Limited · Phoenix Mill
Thrupp · Stroud · Gloucestershire · GL5 2BU

British Library Cataloguing in Publication Data
A catalogue record for this book is available from the British Library.

ISBN 0-7509-3396-8

A detail from the Dingley monument in St Michael and All Angels' Church, Cropthorne. The Dingley family dominated the village for generations.

Typeset in 11/13.5pt Garamond.
Typesetting and origination by
Sutton Publishing Limited.
Printed and bound in England by
J.H. Haynes & Co. Ltd, Sparkford.

INTRODUCTION

In general the vast majority of place-names in Worcestershire come from the Old English tongue introduced to these shores with the coming of the Anglo-Saxons. Old English (also known as Saxon) was the principal language in England from the eighth to the twelfth centuries, when it evolved to what is known as Middle English, which itself began to evolve to the modern form from around the sixteenth century.

More permanent features were named by much earlier inhabitants. Rivers, hills and other geographical features originate from the pre-Roman British languages (related to Welsh, Cornish, Breton, Gaelic) and as such are sometimes difficult to define. Not only are they difficult for us to understand at times, but they were also beyond the understanding of the Saxons, who would often add their own 'hill-name' element to that of the British one, leading to a name that essentially meant 'hill hill'.

There are also some examples of later Welsh influence in Worcestershire in the west of the county, the border with Wales once much further east than it is today. The place-names of the north of England were influenced by the Scandinavian tongues, and although there are a few examples in the county, they are notable exceptions. Double-barrelled place-names invariably have one element (usually the second) which refers to a manorial lord, especially those of the Norman era; hence Old French is another language to have contributed to the county's place-names.

The Romans, despite their undoubted influence on the civilised world for several centuries, contributed virtually nothing to place-names. Many are aware that Roman towns are evidenced today with names ending in -chester and -cester; however this was nothing to do with the Romans, the name-ending coming from the Saxon *caester*, which referred to a Roman town. The Romans were highly adept at absorbing many facets of the lands they conquered. Technologies, cultures, gods, were all taken into their society, and so were place-names, where they simply Latinised the name already in use. (Londinium for London is a prime example, a place-name which continues to defy all attempts at definition.)

As young children we are made aware of the excellent network of roads constructed during the Roman occupation. However, there is reason to believe that the famous straight roads were built on existing trackways which had been in use for centuries before Rome's traditional founding in 753 BC. At this time woodland covered much of the country and the few travellers were certainly at considerable risk of losing their way soon after they lost sight of their departure point. So pathways were marked between the sparse hill-forts of the day, surviving today as the phenomenon known as ley lines. Armed with three staves, men would set off, aligning the third staff with the other two and taking advantage of obvious markers for those who were to follow. Such markers included burial-mounds, fords, places of heathen worship, and permanent geographical features. Clearly, these features could not be relied upon to appear often enough to be always within sight, so artificial markers were constructed – heaped stones, a burnt tree, geometrical figures made from boulders or perhaps parallel tree trunks – anything which stood out and was instantly recognisable. Many place-names which appear to have no logical origins have originated from these markers, Burnt Tree being among the most numerous. (Interestingly, the giant figure cut into the chalk at Cerne Abbas is thought by some to represent those who developed these ancient tracks.)

In order to define a place-name, it is important to find as many early forms of the name as possible. Clearly these ancient documents were all hand-written and have been copied (again by hand) in order to preserve the information. As we are all aware, to copy anything is to invite error – a problem where place-names are concerned, for a difference of just one letter can easily mean a definition is uncertain, unknown, or erroneous.

At Knightwick, on the Worcester road.

This would seem the right moment to comment on the magnificent survey of 1086, the Domesday Book, and its significance when attempting to define place-name origins. That it is a useful tool is undeniable, but it should never be used as a defining source. Remember, the work is written in a form of Latin; the survey itself was carried out principally by Normans who had their origins in Scandinavia and spoke a distinct dialect of Old French; and the vast majority of the population spoke either Old English (a tongue which bears more resemblance to modern German than English) or one of the old Scandinavian tongues (these more closely related to their modern counterparts). The dividing diagonal across England separating the Saxons and the Norsemen meant that Worcestershire was predominantly Saxon-speaking, all of which meant that those carrying out the survey could understand very little of what some inhabitants were saying (even if regional dialects and characteristics are removed from the equation). Hence those who recorded the details were virtually forced to write proper names phonetically, unless they were lucky enough to find that the representative from the Saxon village was literate.

As an example to illustrate the nature of the problem, consider this: if the grey squirrel were to be introduced from North America today, and both the Americans and the English were largely illiterate, despite the fact that we would have the tremendous advantage of speaking the same language, we would be under the impression that this previously unknown yet engaging arboreal rodent was known as a 'skwirl'.

Despite the variety of languages and the many problems which can be encountered, the origin of place-names has proved a fascinating subject for many years (the Venerable Bede wrote extensively on the subject in his *Ecclesiastical History of the English Nation*, published in the eighth century). Defining any name is often open to interpretation by the individual, although a consensus of opinion is usually reached after a time (even if it is simply 'we don't know').

A surprising array of sources has provided the inspiration for the ensuing place-names. Predictably we find topography, water, fauna, animals and individuals; but also we find the seasons, food, pests, sports, and even the American War of Independence.

COMMON PLACE-NAME ELEMENTS

broc	brook, stream	*geat*	gap, pass
burh	fortified place	*halh*	corner of land
burna	stream	*ham*	homestead
caester	Roman stronghold	*hamm*	water meadow
cirice	church	*holt*	wood, thicket
clif	cliff, slope, or bank	*hyll*	hill
cnoll	hill-top	*hyrst*	wooded hill
cot	cottage	*leah*	woodland glade
cumb	valley (particularly a short valley)	*port*	market place
		stan	stone
dael	valley	*stoc*	secondary, or special place
denu	valley	*stow*	assembly place
dic	ditch	*throp*	hamlet
dun	hill	*tun*	farmstead, village
eg	island, dry ground in marshland	*wella*	spring, stream
		wic	specialised farm (especially dairy)
feld	tract of land cleared of trees		
fenn	marsh	*worthig*	enclosed settlement
ford	river-crossing		

St Peter's Church, Inkberrow.

Abberley

The Domesday Book lists Abberley, located 11 miles south-west of Stourport, as *Edboldelege*, while entries from 1180 and 1216 gives *Aldoldelega* and *Abbedeslegh* respectively. Here the name points to an origin of 'woodland clearing of a man called Eadbeald', with the personal name preceding the Saxon or Old English word *leah*. This can refer either to a natural glade in the extensive woodlands of the Saxon era or, more commonly, a man-made one, usually from many years before the Anglo-Saxons arrived on our shores in the fifth century AD.

Abberley was under the control of Ralph de Tosny in 1086. He was one of the major landholders following the Norman Conquest. Also known as Ralph de Conches, his lands extended over seven counties across the southern half of

Abberley village sign, with Clows Top in the background.

The Manor Arms with its array of heraldic shields.

England. Already a powerful man in his own right, his influence was assured with the marriage of his sister Adeline to Earl William FitzOsbern, who was to act as regent alongside Odo of Bayeux in the absence of the king. It is doubtful if he ever saw Abberley, although he certainly spent plenty of time in neighbouring Herefordshire where he was Lord of Clifford Castle.

During the last century a workman repairing the ruined wall of the nave found five silver spoons hidden in a crevice of the Norman church.

Near Abberley is **Apostles Oak**. Oak trees were revered by the Druids and, as is often the case, the same places of worship were utilised by later religions. (This makes perfect sense if one considers that the congregation would have been used to meeting in there, and the new religion, Christianity, effectively evicted the previous belief as physically as possible.) Traditionally, Apostles Oak was one of several claimed to be the meeting place of the Synod of St Augustine and the clergy in 603. However, the written account puts the meeting place on the borders of the Hwiccian and West Saxon kingdoms, which would give a location a little south of Bath in Wiltshire. Yet there is no reason to doubt that news of this meeting was delivered to the Christians who gathered here shortly afterward.

One local name is somewhat obscure. **Meaneatt Wood** certainly takes its second element from the Saxon *geat* meaning 'gap, or pass', but the first element remains obscure. One John Meneye is recorded as being in residence in 1327 and it is possible the place-name is taken from the family name, although the reverse is also as likely.

Abberton

The Saxon -*tun* is possibly the most common element in English place-names, most often seen today as -ton. Not surprisingly the meaning can be as simplistic as merely 'settlement' when appearing on its own, or as part of surprisingly detailed information when found with other elements.

Situated 12 miles north-east of Pershore, Domesday lists the name as *Edbretintune*, the spelling of which is crucially different from the earlier record of 972 as *Eadbrihtincgtun* which, somewhat unusually, is identical to the post-Domesday record dated 1282. This then is 'the settlement of the people of Eadbeorht', consisting of three elements: the 'personal name', Saxon -*inga*-, and -*tun*. Other than what the name clearly states, we can also deduce that Eadbeorht may well have never lived here. As the name states, it was Eadbeorht's people who made this their home and, although we can never be certain, who may have come here to begin a new settlement when the original 'Eadbeorht's place' was either too crowded or could not support the increase in population.

Ab Lench

Sitting at the mid-way point between Inkberrow and Evesham, and known as Abbots Lench as recently as the late nineteenth century, early listings are found as *Aberleng* (DB) and *Abbelench* (1227) which is derived from Saxon *hlenc*, a side-form of *hlinc* and related to the Norse *hlanki* meaning 'hill'. That it refers to higher ground here is unquestionable, although the exact meaning of *hlinc* remains uncertain. The additional first element clearly refers to possession of this land by the church, being added to differentiate from other settlements known as Lench nearby.

Abbots Morton

This community south of Inkberrow was, like Abbots Lench, the property of the church soon after the Norman Conquest. Here the Bishop of Evesham was responsible for overseeing the administration of the settlement. Domesday's *Mortune* is little different from the earliest known record of this place as *Mortun*, which shows two Saxon words: *mor* and *tun*, giving a graphic description of 'the settlement by a fen, or marshy ground'.

The comparative safety of this village afforded a refuge for those attempting to avoid raids from the outlaws who lived in Feckenham Forest.

Aldington

There are just two significant records of this place west of Evesham in historical documents: as *Aldintona* in 709 and *Aldintone* in 1086. While these examples are by no means conclusive, we can be fairly certain of the personal name as 'the settlement of Ealda's people'.

Alfrick

Two thirteenth-century listings as *Alcredeswike* and *Alfrewike* point to the origins of Alfrick, 6 miles west of Worcester, as 'Ealhred's wic'. The Saxon *wic* refers to a farming community.

Lucknalls Farm preserves a Saxon name used to refer to 'an enclosed spring'. 'Enclosed' could suggest a well was constructed here, although we would expect to find the Saxon *wella*. Therefore the probable sense here is 'having no run-off, creating a pool', possibly after the building of a dam.

The name of **Oughton Wells** is another of Saxon or Old English origins, here meaning '(place at) the farm by the hill'. The region known as **Yarringtons** is, as we would expect, a later personal name: William Yarrington is known to have been a tenant in 1649, although it is likely that the family had been here for some time before this.

The crossroads at Alfrick.

Alton

Domesday's *Alvintune* bears more resemblance to the modern name than it does to *Eanulfintun* which is found in 1023, just sixty-three years earlier. Today the Saxon *-inga-* element has been lost entirely, but the earlier versions clearly point to this place being 'the settlement of Eanwulf's people'.

The Domesday survey reveals this village to be among the extensive lands of Ralph de Tosny (*see* Abberley).

Alvechurch

This town was once a settlement which grew up around 'the church of Aelfgyth', as evidenced by the tenth-century listing as *Aelfgythe cyrcan* and a century later as *Alvievecherche*. The Saxon *cirice* is a fairly common element in place-names, although the personal name is quite rare as it is a woman's name. Female leaders were uncommon enough, but to find one associated with a church is so unusual the two elements may well date from different eras and thus are not directly related other than as a name. Archaeological evidence has been found here of an episcopal palace, together with a defensive moat and fishponds which were maintained to provide food for the community.

What is now known as **Wast Hills** is recorded as two places, verified from the eighth- and ninth-century records of *aet Waersetfelda, Wearsetfeld, Werstfeld* and *Waersethyll.* Old English *weardsetl-feld* and *-hyll* here refer to 'cleared land with a watch-tower' or 'hill with a watch-tower'. Presumably the look-out point was on the hill, with the *feld* close by.

Outside Alvechurch in the direction of Redditch we find three names with a common element: **Brockhill Dingle**, **Brockhill Farm** and **Brockhill Wood**. The first would have been the original name meaning 'the brook in the hollow', a dingle is a low-lying strip of land, usually featuring water in some form (particularly one that is seasonal). The other additions are self-explanatory.

There is a minor tributary of the River Arrow here, known as the **Alve**. This is certainly one of the examples of a river-name derived from back-formation from the place-name (the reverse is normally true). We can also be fairly certain that the original river-name would have been in use up until at least the tenth century, as the 'Alve-' element of Alvechurch is not seen until then. Sadly no record of the earlier name exists today.

On 10 December 1361, during the reign of Edward III, Brian, Bishop of Worcester and Chancellor of England died as a result of the Black Death. This powerful and influential man lived in Alvechurch for some of his life, and it was here that he heard from Edward, the Black Prince, the news of the English victory over the French at Poitiers. There are no place-names commemorating the man himself, but the disease which ravaged Britain and Europe in the thirteenth century has left its mark in **Pestilence Lane**.

Coach and Horses is a common pub name popular from the seventeenth century, as inns were natural stopping places for passengers and horses, providing the chance of refreshment and rest.

Arley, Upper and Lower

Historical listings include *Earnleie* in 996, and in Domesday as *alia Ernlege* and *Emlege*. This is from two Saxon elements *earn-leah* giving 'wood where eagles are found'. A later listing as *Arnleg* in 1232 confirms this, although this record refers specifically to the wood itself, not the village. The two settlements north of Bewdley were quite possibly settled at virtually the same time by the same people. However, it may be that the two grew independently as there is just enough space between to give them both sufficient land to survive. That the names are identical is unremarkable, while the additions which differentiate between the two are self-explanatory.

Armscott

Another common Saxon place-name ending is *cot*. From 1042 we find the record of *Eadmundescotan* giving us 'Eadmund's cottages'. That the place was referred to as 'cottages' rather than a 'settlement' may suggest that the inhabitants were employed elsewhere, rather than being a self-sustained farming community. Without knowing what labours the people were required for, there can be no possibility of ever knowing for certain.

Arrow, River

Rising in the Lickey Hills, the course of this river has often marked the border between the county and neighbouring Warwickshire over the centuries. The origin, as with so many river-names, is Celtic (possibly even pre-Celtic) and is related to that of the Avon into which it flows. This river does not resemble an arrow either in shape or in the sense 'as straight as an arrow'; the name simply means 'stream'.

Astley

The eleventh-century records of this place south of Stourport-on-Severn as *Aestlaeh* and *Eslei* confirm this is 'eastern woodland clearing'. Often names containing a direction point out that the place was originally a satellite

St Peter's Church, Astley, in early summer.

community of a larger settlement, normally to aid agricultural efficiency, or simply to act as a storehouse, although it may have been simply a natural woodland clearing to the east of another settlement or on the eastern side of the area of woodland.

Domesday records that Astley was part of the lands of Ralph de Tosny (*see* Abberley), and for a small place had a surprising four watermills. Carvings dating from the Norman era have survived to the present.

Here is a raised area of land known as **The Burf**. This unusual name is easily defined, and enables us a glimpse of at least a part of the inhabitants' lives, as this is 'the raised land topped by a meeting place'. Hence this was almost certainly the venue of the moot, the meeting of the local administrators and/or their representatives for the local hundred (a sub-division of the counties).

Another local name is that of **Larford**, which is another of the descriptive Saxon names. Here we find 'the (place at) the ford where wild iris grows'.

Aston Fields

Found as *Eastun* in 767, this is clearly 'the eastern settlement'. Here we can be certain it was an outlying settlement for agricultural purposes (*see* Astley), as evidenced by the addition of 'Fields'. As the Domesday survey shows this settlement must have been a prosperous place in the eleventh century, for there

Place-names both local and further afield.

were two mills here. All Domesday's mills refer to watermills and the two here would have provided a decent income for the landholders of Worcester Cathedral.

Aston Magna

Occurring as *Estona* in 1209, the name is identical in origin with that of Aston Fields except this was a larger settlement as shown by the addition of 'Magna'.

Atch Lench

Found 5 miles north of Evesham, the second element of this place-name is identical with that of Ab Lench, while the addition comes from the early Norman tenant Randulf, here shown as a pet form of the name. The family must have taken the manor fairly early in the Norman era, for Domesday shows the name as *Achelenz*, which had evolved into *Aches Lenche* by 1262. The eleventh-century survey shows this settlement was held jointly by the churches of Worcester and Evesham, who would have received a tidy annual sum from the production of honey and from the working watermill here.

Avon Bank

Listed as *Afon* in 704 and *Afene* in 780, this is one of the most common river-names in the British Isles. From Old British (of the pre-Roman era) it is related to Welsh *afon*, Cornish *avon*, and Irish *abhann* and means simply 'river'. Perhaps to refer to the local water course as such may seem rather simplistic but it is by no means surprising. Even today individuals rarely refer to the local river or stream by name but as 'the river'.

The addition of 'Bank' is self-explanatory.

B

Badsey

Listed as *Baddeseia* in 709 and *Badesei* in Domesday, when it was held by the church of Evesham just 2 miles west of here. this name tells us of 'Baeddi's island'. The term 'island' is a little misleading for it would be unlikely to refer to an island as we would know it today; more likely it refers to an area of higher ground in a marshy area. The same man gave his name to a nearby stream which appears as *Baeddeswellan* in 972.

The region of **Aldington** is seen as early as 709 when recorded as *Aldintone*. This is 'the farmstead of the family or followers of Ealda'. Indeed Ealda himself may never have lived here; this could easily have been a smaller overspill settlement founded by Ealda's people.

Barnt Green

Today a part of the West Midlands, the first element here comes from an Old English word *bernet*. Although rarely found on its own, it is a reasonably common element in place-names and denotes 'a wooded place cleared by burning'. Evidence has been found of a great fire here in the remote past. This may have been a natural event following a lightning strike, an attempt which got out of control, to clear the scrub from a clearing, or a deliberate decimation of the trees over a large area. While either of the first two are plausible, the third seems unlikely as this was not typical Saxon practice.

Bayton

The two historical forms here are *Beitone* in 1080 and Domesday's *Betune*, when one Rayner acted as lord of the manor on behalf of Ralph de Tosny, ensuring maximum productivity on its single watermill. Neither of these forms is accurate enough to decide if the personal name is 'Baege or Baega's farming settlement', which, although very similar, are the male and female forms of the name respectively.

Shakenhurst is another name of Saxon origins describing '(the settlement at) Sceacca's wood'. The manor-house of the region known as **Culverness** derives its name from the Saxon for 'dove's nest'. This should not be taken literally. place-names should identify the specific place, and an individual nest is neither particularly noticeable nor a permanent landmark. Clearly this 'nest' is a reference to the number of birds found here, which tells us there must have been a reliable and plentiful food supply in order to maintain a substantial population year after year.

Belbroughton

Originally two distinct villages east of Kidderminster: Bell and Broughton. The former, seen as *Beolne* in 817, *Bellen* in 1086, and *Belne* in 1212, is an old river-name listed as *Beolne* in 1300, and is itself from the Saxon *beolone* meaning 'henbane' which presumably grew here in abundance. The earliest record of Broughton is as *Brocton* in 817, easily seen as 'the farmstead on the brook'.

Belbroughton was held by Countess Godiva prior to the Norman Conquest and Urso d'Abitot after it. Godiva, best remembered for her legendary naked ride through the streets of Coventry, was the wife of Leofric, Earl of Mercia, the sister of Thorold, and grandmother of Edwin and Morcar who followed her example and rebelled against the Norman regime in later years. This settlement was renowned for making excellent scythes, which were in great demand by neighbouring communities.

Pepper Wood here has a name whose origins are closely connected with that of **Peopleton**. Early forms include *Pupperode* (1230) and *Pipperod* (1262), which point to the personal name Pyppa. Indicative of the proximity to the Welsh border, the place-name of **Dordale** has a Welsh first element *dwfr* and a second Saxon element *dael*, literally meaning 'water dale'. Today we find the place-names of **Dordale Farm**, **Dordale Green** and **Dordale Brook** on local maps.

The earliest signs for taverns were simple roadside indications to travellers that such was available (*see* Bromsgrove). Doubtless many a sheaf of barley or hop-vine became dislodged, so it is easy to see how the name of the landmark came into use by the locals, referring to where ale could be obtained. The **Hollybush** is today associated with Christmas, which was certainly inherited from the Roman festival of Saturnalia, abandoned in favour of Christmas when the Romans adopted Christianity – thus fixing the date of Yuletide.

With over a hundred pubs throughout England named after the legendary outlaw Robin Hood, the name seems to have spread in the nineteenth century as the Ancient Order of Foresters opened new courts or lodges. It is likely that the sign represented the order and, being thought to resemble he of Sherwood Forest, became the nickname of the inn. Very soon the popularity would have spread, particularly when inn-keepers used the following rhyme as an invitation to prospective customers:

> You gentlemen and yeomen good,
> Come in and drink with Robin Hood.
> If Robin Hood not be at home,
> Come in and drink with Little John.

Bengeworth

Listed in the tenth century as *Benningcuuyro* and *Bynnyncgwyro*, and *Beningeorde* in Domesday, this is derived from the Saxon word *worth*. This referred to a farming settlement with a wooden palisade, designed to keep livestock from straying or from predators rather than to defend the inhabitants as it would have done in earlier times. The first element comes from a personal name, giving 'the farming settlement of Beonna's people'.

It may seem strange to find any mention of a port this far inland; however to the Saxons a port was simply 'a market' irrespective of its location. Hence the name of **Port Street** indicates the site of an early marketplace.

Bentley

This is a fairly common name in England, usually found with a second element for distinction. Here the Saxon *beonet-leah* is seen in the tenth-century listing as *Beonetlaeage*, which is 'the woodland clearing overgrown with bent grass'.

Towards the end of the eleventh century these lands were part of the vast holdings of Urso d'Abitot in the county, which led to him being known as Urso of Worcester. His importance in the county during the troubled times following the Norman Conquest cannot be overstated. He was instrumental in subduing the revolt of Roger of Hereford in 1075, together with his efforts in maintaining the smooth and efficient administrative processes of Worcestershire. Brother of Robert the Bursar, Sheriff of Worcestershire, he took much land from Worcester church and Odo, Bishop of Bayeux, the half-brother of William the Conqueror. That Urso's efforts were appreciated is clear as he was given lands that had once belonged to Odo, who had acted as co-regent in the king's absence, but had been imprisoned in Rouen by 1086 for his role in plotting against the new establishment.

Bentley Pauncefote

As noted in the entry for Bentley this is 'the woodland glade overgrown with bent grass'. Listed as *Beneslei* in Domesday, *Benetlega* in 1185, and *Benetleg Pancevot* in 1212, the additional element refers to the landlord Richard Panzeuot who held the manor in 1185. Furthermore, we know this to be a Norman nickname meaning 'round belly'. So in defining the place-name we are also given a reasonable facsimile of the man at the helm at the end of the twelfth century, a man who would otherwise have been just a name.

The Thrift is an unusual name, which has two possible origins: either the plant known as thrift, or more likely a corruption of Old English *frith* meaning 'wood where scrub grows'.

Beoley

Ever since the earliest species of the hominid first climbed down from the trees (and probably before) honey has been an important dietary supplement. The minimal dangers of collection are far outweighed by the benefits of this natural food. No surprise that the insects themselves have left their mark on the maps of England then, and Beoley, north of Redditch, is just one of many examples across the land. The Saxon spelling was *beo*, although pronounced the same as today. Listed as *Beoleah* in 972 and *Beolege* in Domesday, this is 'the woodland clearing where bees are to be found'. Beoley was part of the land held by Pershore church before and after the Norman Conquest.

Gorcott Hill is another name of Old English derivation. The additional 'hill' is a pointer that the name did not originate from the hill itself. Indeed early listings show this name means 'cottages at the muddy place'. No record survives of the earlier name applied to the hill, only early forms of the present name indicating that the cottages were nearby.

Berrington Green

Historical documents record this place as *Beritune* and *Biriton* in 1086 and 1275 respectively, Domesday also noting that this was land held by Osbern FitzRichard, who had inherited it from his father. This is the Saxon or Old English *Byr(i)gtun* – 'the farming settlement by or belonging to a burg'. The word *burg* has evolved into the common place-name ending today seen as -burh, -burgh, -brough, or -borough. It refers to a hill-fort, a settlement on higher ground with at least one defensive ditch. The Anglo-Saxons would not have excavated the ditch themselves; that would have been done by the people who inhabited our islands prior to the arrival of the Romans. The Saxons were simply making use of a prime site.

The additional 'Green' is self-explanatory and simplistic but necessary owing to similarly named places in nearby Gloucestershire, Herefordshire and Shropshire: an indication of how readily Saxon settlers occupied sites which may well have been uninhabited for five hundred years or more.

Berrow

No historical record exists prior to 1190, when we find *la berge*, *la Berwe* and *Berge* over a period of just thirteen years. This comes from *beorg*, the Saxon word meaning simply 'hill'. In the early forms the references are firstly to the hill itself, while the other two refer to the '(place at) the hill or mound'.

The Admiral Rodney at Berrow.

Besford

Early forms include *Bettesford* in 972, *Beford* in Domesday, and *Bezceford* in 1176, pointing to an origin of 'ford of a man called Betti'. At the close of the eleventh century the administration of these lands was split between William the Priest, on behalf of Westminster church, and Walter Ponther for Urso d'Abitot.

With the land crossed by numerous watercourses, the absence of more than a handful of bridges meant that crossing-points were at a premium. When attempting to track ley lines (ancient pathways) fording-points are major markers. That these are often aligned across impressive distances in a straight line cannot be coincidental, thus at least some of the crossing-places must have been man-made or, at the very least, man-maintained. To make the crossing of a heavy cart as easy as possible, the bed of the stream was reinforced by rocks, laid to provide an even surface. In return for cutting the journey time down appreciably, a toll would have been paid by travellers, normally in the form of goods which they would already be carrying either to trade or specifically as a toll fee.

Bewdley

Despite the concrete which now covers much of Bewdley, it is still possible to see why this town in the Severn Valley derives its name from the Old French for 'beautiful place'. Early forms include *Beuleu* in 1275, *Buleye* 1315, *Beudle* 1335, and *Beaudele* in 1335. It seems highly unlikely that such a desirable site would have evaded settlement until the thirteenth century, although just what earlier settlers knew the area as is unknown and will doubtless remain a mystery.

Bewdley's industries have included a flourishing trade in products made from horn, including drinking-cups, combs, snuff-boxes and lanterns, all of which lasted until the beginning of the twentieth century when other materials became more sought after. Another trade which suffered from a diminishing demand was that of the manufacture of cloth caps. Until comparatively recently very few locals were ever seen out without some form of headgear. Indeed, two centuries ago people of the district were compelled to wear one in support of their local industry or face a fine of 3s 4d (worth noting today when consumers are urged to 'Buy British').

That **Bannutt** is found only in Worcestershire as a place-name gives a clue as to its origins. Aside from **Bannutt Tree Farm** near Bewdley, there is a similar farm at

Bewdley town centre.

A variety of architectural types, rnstling on the banks of the Severn.

Chaseley and a **Bannutt Hill** near Kempsey, all of which derive from a Midlands dialect word *bannutt*. The etymology of the word is unknown, but is certainly something akin to 'bone nut' or 'nut with a bone-like shell' and used to refer specifically to the walnut tree or its fruit.

Crundels Farm would seem to be a personal name, but the 's' is not personal nor plural but a minor corruption. Old English *crundel* is one of those words from the Germanic language group which give a good deal of information, despite only having seven letters. Thus the origins as 'a ravine or dividing strip, always in a dip and with running water for at least some of the year', creates a reasonable image of this region as it would have been in the latter half of the first millennium AD. While this did not begin as a personal name, it is entirely possible that it became a family name in later years and may well explain the additional 's'.

Tickenhill is derived from the Old English for 'the kid's hill', which presumably refers to the young of the goat. However, the young of the roebuck is also called a kid, and this creature would have been seen frequently as numbers were much greater.

Bark Hill led from the Wyre Forest towards the tanneries, of which there were once eight alongside the river at Bewdley, bark being used in the tanning process. **Lax Lane** refers to the salmon fall at the bottom of the lane, *lax* being the Old Scandinavian term for salmon. Most towns have a High Street, usually used in the sense of 'the main street'. However it is possible that Bewdley's version refers to the fact that it stood above the larger part of the town, which was often waterlogged. **Load Street** was where cargo was loaded on to boats, while **Coles Quay** enabled coal from Highley to be transported along the river.

Other street-names include **Pewterers' Alley**, named from the trade; **Rag Lane**, where ragwort grew unchecked; and **Welch Gate** which marks the passageway to the road leading to Wales. **Dog Lane** was formerly known as **Duck Lane**, which some sources suggest is a reference to a ducking-stool, but more likely to be the less fanciful waterfowl. The modern form is simply a corruption.

The **Cock and Magpie** is a typical pub name, most of those today taken from the long list of names instantly recognisable as referring to a public house. In medieval times peacock pie was an ostentatious dish for the wealthy. Premises where such was available were named accordingly, the corruption of which appears today as the Cock and Magpie. The name would have had a different meaning for the commoners too. In Elizabethan times 'by Cock and pie' was an oath where 'cock' was a euphemism for God and 'pie' the rule-book of the Catholic Church.

Birlingham

Names ending in -ham are widespread, not surprisingly, considering two Old English words have contributed. Here the origin is *hamm*, which is used to refer to a water meadow or land where water plays a significant (sometimes seasonal) role in the lives of the settlement. Listed as *Byrlingahamm* in 972 and *Berlingeham* in Domesday, Birlingham (south of Pershore) was originally 'the land of the family or followers of a man called Byrla'. The personal name itself is thought to be derived from *Byrgla* and may well be a nickname.

Domesday notes the land was divided between Westminster church and Urso d'Abitot, both presumably benefiting from the fishery here.

Birtsmorton

Most names containing a distinctive addition appear today as double-barrelled but Birtsmorton is one of the exceptions. Records list this place simply as *Mortun* in 1235 and as *Brittesmoretone* thirty-one years earlier. Many Mortons are distributed throughout England, from Saxon *mor-tun*, 'the settlement by a fen or wetland' with this particular village belonging to the family of le Bret from the twelfth century. The name Bret means 'Breton', a native of the region of France known as Brittany who spoke a language very closely related to Welsh, Cornish and Old British.

Bishampton

Listed as *Bisantune* in Domesday and with fourteenth-century records of *Bishamtone* and *Bisshopeshampton*, this was once thought to have been 'the settlement or homestead belonging to the bishop'. However, these comparatively late forms are probably misleading for this place midway between Pershore and Inkberrow was certainly a thriving community prior to the Norman Conquest, as evidenced by the Domesday entry. The great survey lists the village as being part of the extensive lands of Worcester Cathedral and managed by one Roger de Lacy and two (unnamed) Frenchmen, with the major asset a watermill. This has added further weight to a connection with the Bishop of Worcester in the past. More recent thinking has tended to discount the earlier definition in favour of 'homestead of a man called Bisa', who probably ran the mill prior to the lands falling under the control of the bishopric.

Blackmore

Even without the record of *Blakemor* in 1314, there is no doubting the name means 'the black moor'. This refers to the dark soil rather than the vegetation.

Blackwell

Situated north-east of Bromsgrove, this place is, as with Blackmore, a name of undisputed origin in 'black stream', seen as *Blacwaelle* in 964. The stream would have appeared dark because of the observer owing to the colour and/or depth of the bed, not, as is sometimes thought, because of the colour of the water. This would have been the sole source of all the settlement's water and no settlement would have been founded alongside an undrinkable water supply.

Blockley

As evidenced by the listings as *Blocclea* in 1320, *Blochlei* in 1186, and *Bloccanleeh* in 855, this village east of Broadway has a name which comes from 'Blocca's woodland clearing'. This is assuming that Blocca is a personal name, although no written evidence of this name has ever been found.

The Old English elements of **Draycot** are *draeg-cot*, 'the cottages by a portage'. A rarely used word today, portage describes a region of land between two river systems where boats and/or cargo was transported (literally 'dragged') overland to cut down on travelling time.

While the **Great Western Arms** is a clear reference to the railway, the name may not have been derived from the line built by Isambard Kingdom Brunel, but by an early landlord who had associations with the most famous of the old railway companies, which featured engines in green livery.

Bockleton

As there are no listings prior to Domesday's *Boclintun* or as *Boclinton* in the late twelfth century, the first element of Bockleton is uncertain. It is tempting to simply opt for the most obvious origin in Saxon *boc-hlinc-tun*, 'the farmstead by the hill where beech trees grow'. However, such combinations are not often seen. The general region was once home to the tribe known as the Boccelingas, their name being derived from the personal name Boccel or Beoccel. If archaeological evidence could be found that this tribe did live on or around a hill here then this would certainly confirm these people as the origin of the name. This domain remained the property of the Bishop of Hereford following the Norman Conquest.

Local place-names include **Quinton**, a fairly common name which has a number of origins. Ancient listings show this to be of Old English derivation for 'the farmstead of the family or followers of a man called Cwena'. There is also the strangely named **Gettes Ashbed**, a name of interesting etymology, for the manorial affix appears at the front instead of at the end as with nearly all double-barrelled place-names. Without even looking at early records it can be seen that this 'backwards' place-name is clearly of comparatively recent origins. Most manorial names are Norman, or of the Norman French era, which means the name is given as that of **Bentley Pauncefote** which, as we have seen earlier in this chapter, is a 'place at the clearing with bent grass belonging to a man called Panzeuot'. The French language would have given this word order, whereas English (or Old and Middle English) would reverse this order. Hence this name is of Middle English origin in 'the place of ash trees' (literally 'bed'), which was the domain of one John Gette from 1642.

Bow Brook

Not as obvious as we would think: the 'bow' does not refer to a bend in the meandering stream. The name comes from Old English *boga*, which in general use means 'bridge' but is also specifically used to refer to 'an arched bridge'. We can safely assume that local usage has retained the original meaning and this is one of the few freshwater courses to take a name from something only indirectly related to the brook itself, in this case a footbridge.

Bradley

Featuring two of the most common elements in English place-names, taken from *brad-leah* '(place at) the wide woodland clearing', it is rather unusual to find Bradley standing alone. Normally the name represents the end of a longer name featuring a personal name. This village east of Droitwich seems to be the exception, for even with early forms as *Bradanlaeh* and *Bradanleage* from 730 and

The Fox Inn at Bransford has a delightful pub sign.

803 respectively there is still no evidence that any personal name ever contributed (unless it was lost at a very early stage).

At the time of Domesday the settlement belonged to Worcester church, with Archdeacon Alric the nominated figurehead.

Bransford

Recorded as *Bregnesford* in 963 and *Bradnesforde* in Domesday, the first element was once thought to refer to a burial-mound; however, no evidence remains that such ever existed. Although we do find an entry from 1107 of *Bragenmonna broc* which may suggest the origin to be Old English or Saxon *braegen*, literally meaning 'brain', it is used here in the sense of 'crown, or head of the hill'. The brook's source is the hill, while Bransford grew up from the crossing-point, or ford south-west of Worcester. Bransford, together with its profitable watermill, was among the extensive holdings of the church in Worcestershire which were taken by Urso d'Abitot.

Bredicot

Bradigocotan, *Bradingcotan* and *Bradecote* are found in the ninth, tenth and eleventh centuries respectively and, although the personal name is somewhat open to interpretation, this place was once 'the cottages of the family or followers of Brada'.

As with Besford, Walter Ponther acted as landlord for Worcester church at the time of Domesday, while the woodland was king's land. Although there is no evidence of a Roman settlement here, coinage of that era has been found here, suggesting it may have been a temporary Roman encampment.

Bredon

Located south-west of Evesham, the place Bredon lies close to the hill from which it takes its name. Several hill-names in England have three elements derived from three eras and three languages. Here Celtic *bre*, Saxon *dun*, and the modern hill combine to give Bredon Hill. Yet all three elements mean exactly the same thing, giving an origin of 'hill hill hill'. The hill still shows signs of Iron Age fortifications, a prime site with views over fourteen counties.

Early forms of the name include *Breodun in Huic* in 772, *Breodun* in 841, *Breoduninga gemaere* in 984, and Domesday's *Breodun*. The earliest of these gives additional information of what we would have found in the late eighth century, speaking of 'Bredon in the territory of the Hwicce'. These people were a large and successful tribe who settled across a region encompassing parts of Gloucestershire, Worcestershire and Warwickshire. Early forms of the tribal name are found as *prouincia Huicciorum* in 730, *Hwiccium* in 800, and *Hwicca maego* from around the end of the ninth century.

Bredons Norton

For the origins of the first element, see Bredon. The 'north tun, or farmstead' was almost certainly a satellite settlement of the original Saxon Bredon. It is quite possible that this secondary residence grew from what had started out as little more than a haven for livestock or simply a storage facility. The estate of **Norton Park** here was the home of Thomas Copley, a companion of Sir Walter Raleigh on his voyage to America in the late sixteenth century.

Bretforton

Several early records of this name are found east of Evesham, including *Bretfertona* in 709, *Brotfortun* in 714, *Bradferdtuna* in 860, *Bratfortune* in 1086, and the modern form which appears as early as 1275. Had there been a lesser number of historical entries, it is likely the definition would have been thought of as 'farmstead at the broad ford'. However this is most certainly Saxon *bred-ford-tun*, 'the farmstead provided with planks'. The planks may refer to a simple footbridge, or could have been laid along the bed of the river to make it easier for heavy wheeled traffic to cross. Either way the ford would certainly have required constant maintenance and a toll would have been levied on travellers.

As the Domesday survey indicates, Bretforton came under the extensive holdings of Evesham church, when the watermill would have provided a welcome income.

Bricklehampton

As we have seen in other examples, it was commonplace for two settlements in close proximity to share a name. Bricklehampton, west of Evesham, is something of an oddity in that the two known forms, *Brihtulfingtun* in 972 and *Bricstelmestune* in 1086, when it was under the control of Westminster church, seem to be based on different personal names, Beorhtwulf and Beorhthelm. There is no reason to assume either historical record is in error, which leaves but two possible answers to the conundrum: first that there was a deliberate change of name, which seems highly unlikely as this does not occur without a major change in tenants – something which simply did not happen following the Norman Conquest. The only other explanation is that there were originally two settlements, which either grew to form a single village or one of which was abandoned and is now lost. Whichever, it is unlikely we will ever know if this is 'farmstead of the people of Beorhtwulf' or 'Beorhthelm's farmstead'.

Broadwas

Domesday's *Bradewesham* differs slightly from the eighth-century records of *Bradeuuesse* and *Bradewassan*, in that it contains the additional Saxon *ham*

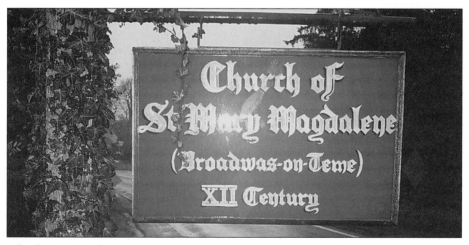

Church sign at Broadwas.

'homestead'. The earlier forms are undoubtedly Old English *brad-waesse*, 'broad tract of alluvial land', which tells us their agricultural land was subject to seasonal flooding, only to be expected west of Worcester and the Severn, and of benefit as the waters deposited silt across the land, replenishing vital soil minerals.

At the end of the eleventh century Worcester church held these lands, a profitable site with two watermills and a fishery which it shared with Hallow. The composer Edward Elgar was born near here in 1857.

Broadway

While the origins of '(place at) the broad way or road' may seem a little too simplistic, there can be no doubt that *Bradanuuege* and *Bradeweia* from 972 and 1086 confirm this definition, the Domesday entry showing this to be under the control of the church at Pershore.

Even without archaeological evidence we can deduce from this that the area was settled long before the Romans arrived, around the time when the first tracks were marked across Britain. Now if woodland proliferated across the land, only crossed with any degree of confidence by means of these trackways, it is clear that these paths would have been narrow, single-track paths. Anything larger would have been pointless, for the population of the entire country was less than that of a medium-sized modern town and travel was only attempted when trading a surplus

The Broadway Hotel.

The Lygon Arms, Broadway.

A charming historic house in Broadway.

for essentials in short supply. Hence a 'broad way' would have been instantly recognisable as the exception and what may be initially considered simplistic is in actual fact very logical.

Tuck Mill Farm is more than a name and gives an insight into the trade here in Saxon times. A tuck mill was a term used to describe a fulling or cloth mill (the mill being water-driven). The **Crown and Trumpet Inn** in Church Street takes both elements from the monarchy; the Crown is clear while the Trumpet refers to the royal herald who was seen on the occasion of a royal visit to the town.

Bromsgrove

Usually this suffix is only found with smaller place-names, such as those of fields or possibly a district, areas comparable in size to the original settlements. However, Bromsgrove has never outgrown its name, having evolved from *Bremesgrefan* in 812, *Bremesgraf* in 822, and *Bremesgrave* in Domesday, still retaining its identity as 'the grove or copse of a man called Breme', from the Saxon *graefe* or *graf*. One imagines he would be quite proud of how much his little settlement has grown over the years and still manages to honour his efforts of anything up to fifteen centuries ago.

Domesday's entry for Bromsgrove shows the town to have been a prosperous one at the close of the eleventh century. Three working mills, four hawks' eyries, and six lead vats for the boiling of brine provided a good income for the king, as well as for those who lived here.

Although early forms of **Apes Dale** are unknown, leading us to believe this is a relatively late name dating from no earlier than the Middle Ages, there can be no doubt of the origins here. The name means exactly what it says – this is 'Ape's dale'; not a reference to some hominid 'missing link' of folklore, nor even to a community of primates, native, feral or otherwise. As indicated by the capital letter, this is a personal name – or more accurately a nickname. Just who was this person with the uncomplimentary nickname was, or what resemblance he (or she) bore to any ape, will always remain a mystery. It is worth noting here that 'monkey' is a fairly late addition to the English language, otherwise the name of this place may have borne the name of the less evolved primate with a tail.

West of Bromsgrove is **Badge Court**, home to an Earl of Shrewsbury for many years. The name is a contraction of the original Saxon *baece-cot*, 'the cottage (or cottages) in the valley'. Not far from here are **Battlefield Farm** and **Battlefield Brook**, both traditionally said to be the sites of minor skirmishes between the warring factions who met in earnest at the Battle of Worcester.

Bungay Lake Farm features the obsolete word *bungy* which literally meant 'puffed out, protruberant'. Like Apes Dale, this was a hardly complimentary term applied to a local man. While it seems the place took its name from a person (or

Boundary marker erected by the Bromsgrove Society to celebrate the Golden Jubilee of Queen Elizabeth II in 2002.

as here his character), there is a slight possibility that the reverse is the case, when the sense would be 'inflated, expanding'.

Early forms of **Catshill** do not show if this name is derived from a personal name in 'Caet's hill', or as 'the hill where wild cats abounded'. Records of this place-name show early forms which could be seen as proof of either definition. Hence we turn our attention to other sources and, while it may seem odd to be looking at natural feline behaviour to define a place-name, add what factual evidence we have to the equation. The cat family, with the exception of lions, have always lived an isolated existence. Lions have evolved to live and hunt as a pride in order that they may take advantage of their larger size to tackle larger and more powerful prey, thus avoiding competition from other predators for the smaller antelope which forms the diet of leopards and cheetahs. Any wild cats of Britain would have preyed on rodents, the population of which is governed entirely by the amount of food available irrespective of the number of predators. Indeed the short breeding cycle of these rodents means populations can explode at astonishing rates, and can fall even faster when the food supply is eventually exhausted. Furthermore even if Catshill was infested with rats and mice, and they had access to a constant food supply (such as the storage barns of the human settlement), the territorial instincts of the cats would have made any 'cat community' impossible, which all goes to prove that we should never forget rational thought when defining place-names and should be content to give the meaning solely from written records. To paraphrase the great fictional detective Sherlock Holmes, 'When you have discounted everything which is possible, the impossible must be true' – and so this is '(place at) Caet's hill'.

Charford is somewhat unusual in having the first element from the Saxon *ceorl* (churl) referring to 'a peasant, countryman' (which should be considered to be plural, even though the early forms indicate otherwise).

Hill names often have very ancient origins (as with river-names) in the Celtic tongues of the pre-Roman era. While there is little written evidence of the language, it is closely related to Welsh, Gaelic, Cornish and Breton. The **Lickey Hills** (long known as **Bromsgrove Lickey**) have several origin theories, with two standing out as the most plausible. One supposes this to be an ancient hill name derived from a word related to Welsh *llechi*, meaning 'stones', and Irish and Gaelic *leac*, specifically 'flat stones' – the root word is used to refer to the weathered and exposed rocks of the Lickeys. A second points to the listing as *Lecheye* in 1255, which is Old English for '(place at) the forest enclosure' and suggests the hills became known by the same name as a Saxon settlement here. If the latter is the case, then there was clearly an earlier name for the hills which is now lost. In medieval times this wild region was the constant haunt of highwaymen and footpads, who were not deterred even when occasional capture saw them made an example of at the gallows erected here.

Lowes Hill has more recent origins, being named from a wealthy family who held this land and much more. The Lowe family are recorded as living in Bromsgrove in 1631, but may well have been here many years prior to the seventeenth century.

Spadesbourne Brook has been defined as 'brook where spades were made', with the justification that water and water-power were essential elements in the edge-tool trade. Water would certainly have been an essential, but this hardly seems a rational explanation for a river-name. The brook also flowed through **Padston**, itself derived from 'Padda's farmstead'. In later years the name was corrupted by an initial 'S', as was the brook which took the place-name by back-formation.

The Spadesbourne emerges from underground at **Mearce Lane**. No early records of note survive, but the name comes from either Saxon *mearc* or *mersc*. If *mearc* is the origin it is a reference to the stream marking a 'boundary'; alternatively if *mersc* it points to the 'marshland' on the north and west side of the path.

The Strand is a road running alongside the Spadesbourne Brook, taking its name from the shallow bank (or shore) of the river. Certainly the name existed well before any houses were built here, which disproves the theory that it was named after the famous London thoroughfare.

James I granted the Manor of Bromsgrove to Sir Richard Grobham Howe and John Howe in 1611. Included were 1,000 acres of unenclosed heathland known as *Barneheath*, known today as *Bournheath*. We would expect the first element of the modern name to represent a stream, and indeed there is a stream here, but this is hardly an unexpected feature and does not distinguish this place from other heaths. If there was no intention to differentiate this heath from others, it would doubtless have simply been known as 'the heath'. Clearly either the seventeenth century or the modern name is in error, the question is which? *Barneheath* would suggest a barn once stood on the heath, while Bournheath is 'heath with a stream'. Following the general trends of place-name evolution, the barn form is the correct one.

Some names have strictly local origins. Such is the case with the delightfully named **Two Penny Cake** (pronounced 'tuppeny'). This triangular piece of land stands at the junction of four roads at Bournheath, and is so-named because the plan resembles the shape of the tuppenny cake sold at Bromsgrove fairs.

The long tradition of cloth manufacture in the area is echoed in many place-names, including **Rack Field**. This meadow near the cattle market had a long wooden rack on which woollen goods were hung to dry. The rack stood for many years until it was demolished in 1840.

Seen today as **Long Eye**, this place-name refers to 'the long island'. Saxon *eg* not only refers to land surrounded by water, but also to dry land in a predominantly marshy area. **Lydiate Ash** can be defined as 'a gate set up between pasture and arable land at the ash trees'. Here 'gate' is used in the sense of 'gap' or 'passage', although there may well have been a conventional gate installed at some stage.

The name of **Timberhanger** is derived from 'hanging wood'. That the term 'timber' is used is important as it refers only to trees large enough to be good for building, Anglo-Saxon houses being built largely of wood. That these trees are described as 'hanging' relates to the situation on a hillside.

Finstall appears as *Vinstalstude* in 1295, *Vynestallstede* in 1368, and *Finstal* in 1328, the first record of the modern form. This name is Old English in origin and refers to the salt extraction and refining which the region was renowned for. The manor of Witton in Droitwich was granted the two *salinae* (brine pits) and a *finstallus*, which is the origin of this place-name and refers to a 'place where firewood is stored'. The firewood was used to heat the brine and evaporate the water leaving the desired salt. Records show that 300 cartloads of wood were used to produce 300 measures (known as *mitts*) of salt. Clearly this was a valued settlement which produced a large quantity of salt, an important commodity of the time.

Gannow Green is fast disappearing from today's maps. The name is derived from Old English *gamen-hoh*, 'a place where games were played'. **Gannow Manor**

House was therefore the scene of tournaments and/or sports. James, Earl of Ormond was in residence here during Edward IV's reign and on his death it was inherited by Margaret, his daughter. Margaret and her husband Thomas, who became Earl of Wiltshire and Ormond, were the parents of Anne Boleyn, third wife of Henry VIII and mother of Queen Elizabeth I.

The house that became known as **Monsieur's Hall** was so-called because it was occupied by a man associated with the French nobility. He stayed here as a refugee during and after the French Revolutionary years, 1793–1815.

Historically recorded as *Offa's Well*, *Offad's Well* and **Alfred's Well**, the last name having endured, the three have nominal similarities, yet quite different origins, each having some degree of merit. *Offa's Well* is a corruption of a personal name, probably influenced by the name of the former king of Mercia who had his seat at Tamworth Castle in Staffordshire and whose name is synonymous with the dyke running the length of the border between England and Wales. The real name here is that of the Orford family who were here in the sixteenth century and were said to have occupied the adjoining cottage in the nineteenth century, showing just how easily names become corrupted even in comparatively modern times. However, there is also a record of a man named Alford, who was a bailiff of Bromsgrove. Doubtless the name had some influence, even if it was not the origin. It was known as *Offad's Well* in 1830, which is almost certainly an amalgam of the other alternatives (although not a deliberate one), and by 1840 had become today's Alfred's Well.

The end of **Ednall Lane** was locally known as *Catchem's End*. Indeed there is reason to believe that Ednall was originally Endall, which has the same significance as Catchem. At a time when manorial lawbreakers could attempt to escape punishment simply by escaping the manor, an offender needed only to flee his pursuers to the end of Ednall Lane which marked the start of the bailiwick of neighbouring **Stoke Prior**. Once across the boundary the local constable had no powers of arrest, which gave rise to the local name of Catchem's End (and the presumed 'end-all').

Named to commemorate the new royal house introduced to Britain by the accession of George I on 1 October 1714, **Hanover Street** was not welcomed by all. One prominent gent in Bromsgrove at the time has gone on record as stating this was evidence of the 'invading Hanoverian rats', obviously spoken by a supporter of the Stuart pretenders to the throne who were known as Jacobites.

Hundred House was the site of a large building in medieval times when it was the venue for meetings of the Hundred Courts of Halfshire, later taken as the name of a local public house.

Church Street was formerly named *Holy Lane*, running from the oldest known vicarage and the main road to the church. Although probably the phonetic spelling of the local pronunciation, there is a record as *Ole Lane* from the eighteenth century.

Another place-name of religious beginnings is that of **Red Cross**. Roman Catholics once carried such at the head of their processions, which presumably passed by the crossroads here. Certainly a large round stone in the centre of the road, recorded as being here by 1773, contained a socket which would have allowed such a cross to be positioned here.

Rotten Row was a name once applied to **Stourbridge Street**. As with the same name in London, it was a term applied to a wealthy landowner and a reference to a rotten borough (prior to the parliamentary reform of 1832, a constituency allowed a representative in the House of Commons despite having very few voters). The first workhouse in the town was located here, part of which later became the offices of the East Worcestershire Waterworks Company.

Linthurst is recorded as *Linthouse* in 1783, where we are told that one Thomas Oakes allowed nine beasts to pasture on *the Waste*, off *the Linthouse*, without having grazing rights. For his misdemeanour Mr Oakes was fined and found his cattle impounded. The name of Linthurst recalls the manufacture of linen cloth in the area, a staple industry for many years.

Washing Stocks is clearly a reference to the cloth-making industry, so important to the economy of the region for many years. 'Washing stocks' alludes to the fulling process and probably refers to a fuller's mill here or nearby.

Whetty is a place-name appearing as *le Wetheye* in 1387. This is from the Saxon denoting 'a wet or marshy forest enclosure'. What became **Whetty Lane** was known as *Watery Lane* in 1772.

Whitford, possibly named to differentiate from **Blakeford** at nearby Stoke Prior, appears as *Whyteford* in 1408, 'the white ford', and would have referred to a light-coloured stream bed.

Worms Ash seems a contradictory place-name, for although the ash tree is a common element the idea of worms having any marked or noticeable effect here is improbable. Early records seem to indicate this was originally a personal name and this is therefore something akin to 'Whierm's place at the ash trees'.

Putcheon is a local name of obscure etymology although if, as it seems, it is of comparably recent derivation, we may have one clue as to its origins. This could be a misspelling of 'puntcheon', the cask in which rum was transported from Jamaica. If we suppose that this was used as the sign, and thus name, of an alehouse here, it may be the origin of this unusual name. What is certain is that the arsonists found guilty in 1822 and transported to the penal colonies came to be called 'the putcheon incendiaries', although it is unclear if the name was taken from this place-name.

Peter's Finger is a name given to a cul-de-sac off Worcester Street, a reference to its shape resembling a bent forefinger. It is not known who Peter was, but it is reasonable to assume, if not in residence personally, that he held property here.

Hewell Grange is the Worcestershire residence of the Earl of Plymouth, the name derived from Old English and Middle English for 'high stream'. Prior to the reign of Henry VIII, when it was granted to the Windsor family, this estate was held by the Holyoake family. In 1477 a friend of Mr Holyoake, the famous William Caxton, set up the first printing press in England at Westminster. Caxton is recorded as setting up his second press at Hewell. Descendants of the Holyoake family still live in Bromsgrove.

Staple Hill is recorded as *la Stapel* in 1485, noted as having a conspicuous post which was probably a boundary marker.

Sidemoor was once known as *Scythmore* and *Sidmore*, which described 'a broad marsh'.

The earliest pub signs were simply a sheaf of barley (or any similar natural ingredient associated with the brewing of ale) tied to a roadside tree to indicate to travellers that refreshments were available. It is easy to see how this evolved into the modern pub sign and name, with the **Hop Pole Inn** an example of one of the earliest forms. For many years poles were used to support hop vines, whereas they are trained on to wires today.

Heraldic origins for pub names are easy to spot. Invariably an animal of unexpected hue is taken from the crest of the local landlord. Indeed, the most popular pub name in the land, the **Red Lion**, is the best example, there being almost 700 pubs so named at the last count.

First seen around the middle of the fourteenth century, the **Boar's Head** is linked to the custom of serving the same with an apple in its mouth at the Christmas feast and has long been a popular pub name. The **Hog's Head** is not a reference to the animal, but the large cask of varying capacities used for beers and wines.

The **Crabmill Inn** is a reference to a cider mill, not that cider was ever made from crab apples! This crab is a kind of winch, so called because of the appearance of the projecting arms, and was used to raise the pulp to allow it to drain.

Today the **Cross Inn** is found close by a church; earlier the inn could also have stood at a crossroads. Whatever the origins, many early cross signs were removed because of the disapproval of the Puritans who deemed it inappropriate to display the sign of the cross outside a tavern. The name of the **Golden Cross** public house has the same origins. The additional 'Golden' has little significance and is purely to distinguish this from other 'Cross' pubs.

> Come, my lads, and crown your wishes,
> With glee come crown your greatest joys,
> Come to the Crown and drink like fishes,
> Spend each a crown my jovial boys.

With the name of the **Crown** on every line, this old verse was probably penned by those who wanted to encourage patronage of the Crown (perhaps written in the bar of the Crown at Bromsgrove?). One of the most common of pub names, several factors have contributed to its popularity: easy illustration, relevance to any era, and showing allegiance to the monarch. The last explains why the name virtually disappeared during the time of Cromwell, only to make a spectacular comeback with the Restoration.

A famous mail-coach running between London and Birmingham could have given its name to the **Greyhound Inn**, maybe not as a staging post but as the later abode of one of those who had connections with this early postal carrying service. Alternatively it could represent the dukes of Newcastle, being taken from the coat of arms. The usual clue to a heraldic origin is given by the addition of a colour; however, as a greyhound is already nominally grey (although this has nothing to do with the colour of the dog, the true etymology is unknown) any secondary colour element would have been ignored.

Pubs named Plough are predictably common, and often found as the **Plough and Harrow**, probably the most common distinguishing addition. There are records of the name being in use since the sixteenth century. Clearly of agricultural origin, signs sometimes depict the constellation of Ursa Major (presumably in order to be different, as such origins seem unlikely). A warning to university students: should your local be named the Plough, this is derived from the term 'ploughed': used to describe students who spend too much time drinking and as a consequence fail their exams.

All **Royal Oaks** mark the flight of Charles II who, together with his aide Colonel Carless, hid in the Boscobel Oak at Shifnal following his defeat at the Battle of Worcester by the Parliamentarians in 1651. It is the second most popular name in the land with over 500 examples. Once a popular dish in taverns, the **Shoulder of Mutton** would have been used as a name, a sign, and advertising hoarding: particularly useful if the landlord was also the local butcher!

Broughton Hackett

This village, west of Worcester, comes from Old English broc-tun, this being 'the farmstead on or near a brook' and is a common name. As is often found with common basic names, a second defining element has been added, usually a former manorial tenant as in this case with the Hackett family who were here in the eleventh century, the eponymous family sharing the land with Westminster church, with the Sheriff of Worcester and one Aiulf acting on the behalf of the church.

Mad or not, **The March Hare** public house reflects the curious behaviour of our largest resident lagomorph in the early spring. Doubtless the popularity of the expression, and hence the name, was influenced by the character in Lewis Carroll's *Alice in Wonderland*.

Burcot

This is noted as king's land in Domesday when it lists *Bericote*, which becomes *Byrcote* a century later. Both point to Saxon *byrig-cot*, 'the cottage(s) belonging to the borough', the borough in question being Bromsgrove, a royal borough.

Pikes Pool was the former name of the road which was later occupied by the railway line. It is clearly taken from a pool here and is itself a clear reference to the fauna. In fact there are three pools here; fed by five springs, they can reach a depth of over 12 ft when full – a home to perch, roach and tench as well as pike. The other smaller pools are known as the **Pink Pools**, and stand on the other side of the track.

Bushley

Early records as *Bisclege*, *Biselege*, *Bisselega* and *Busseleg* found over a period of 150 years would suggest that first impressions of any 'bushes' to be found here south-west of Bredon Hill are wrong. However, the first element is still somewhat unclear. It may be a reduction of *biscop*, the Saxon word for bishop giving 'the woodland clearing belonging to the bishop' and Domesday does confirm that this was in the hands of Worcester Cathedral. Domesday does show that this was a dairy farm, for it specifically records a dairymaid as being here in 1086.

Here is **Aggberrow Wood**, the earliest record of which is from 1275 as *Acberge*. The origins here are Old English *ac-beorg* '(place at or by) the hill where oak trees grow'. The estate known as **Pull Court** is derived from a composite of the Saxon and the Old French words both meaning 'pool'.

C

Castle Morton

From Old English *mor-tun*, 'the farmstead by a fen or marshland', Morton is a very common place-name in England. Thus it was often necessary to add a second element to differentiate between them, especially when the two were nearby. The majority of these affixes feature a former landholder, but in this case his abode was used.

Chaddesley Corbett

An uncertain first element for this place midway between Bromsgrove and Kidderminster, which some hold to be Saxon *ceadder*, Welsh *cader* or Celtic

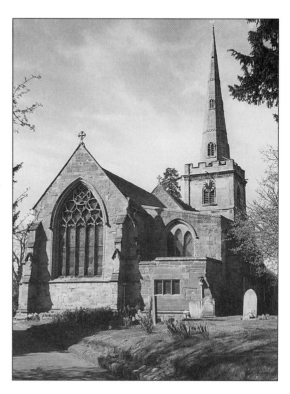

St Cassian's Church, Chaddesley Corbett.

cadeir, all of which refer to the hill. It is possible the name means 'woodland clearing at the hill called Cadeir', the Celtic word referring to a chair-shaped hill, but the likelihood is that the true origins will never be proven, despite finding written examples of *Ceadresleahge* in 816 and *Cedeslai* in 1086.

The manorial addition is less of a mystery. *Chaddesleye Corbett* in 1327 refers to the Corbett family who then held this land. Furthermore we also know Corbett to be an Old French nickname (as well as a personal name) meaning 'raven'.

Prior to the Norman Conquest Chaddesley was held by Aldeva, one of the rare female landholders of the Saxon era. Three watermills here were highly productive, with a tax valuation of twelve packloads of corn annually. **Harvington Hall** near here dates from Tudor times, and has a good collection of period wall-paintings. As a reminder of the political upheavals of the Tudor era and later, the hall also has a maze of secret passages to enable men to beat a hasty and unseen retreat when necessary.

Nearby **Bellington** is a typical Saxon name displaying three elements, 'personal name'-*inga-tun*, giving 'the farmstead of the family or followers of Billa'. As Domesday recalls, this was held by William FitzAnsculf of Picquigny in the Somme region. Son of the Sheriff of Buckinghamshire, he had holdings in twelve counties in the Midlands and west of England, with his seat at Dudley Castle.

The name of **Bluntington** has a different last element from Bellington, despite being identical today. Here the thirteenth-century record as Bluntindon (and others) shows this to be Saxon *dun*, not *tun*. Thus the meaning is '(place at) the hill of the family or followers of Blunt'. The name of **Insetton** comes from Old English *in-saetan* which means 'inhabitants, settlers', probably a reference to an extended family (or families) who moved to set up their own independent settlement.

Towards Bromsgrove is a small woodland area known as **Catpursey Coppice** (some records show the name to be *Cutpercy*). The coppice takes its name from a hamlet *Cutbaldesey*, which was abandoned by the fourteenth century. Today's name is certainly a corruption of the place-name which, in the absence of alternative early forms, is difficult to define. The suffix comes from Saxon *eg*, literally 'island' and used here in the sense 'dry land in a marshy area', which follows an uncertain personal name such as Caedbald or similar.

The delightfully named **Ran Dan Woods** can only be a reference to the noise of the chase, be it in pursuit of wolves, wild boar or deer in the woods. Certainly Celtic in origin the root is uncertain, but was in use throughout the Saxon and Norman eras. During the reign of Edward I, the king commanded Peter Corbett of Chaddesley to rid Worcestershire forests of wolves. It is not known how successful he was, although we do know wolves did not become extinct in England until the end of the eighteenth century.

Archaeologists would be wasting their time hunting for any evidence of any unsteady oak, beech or ash tree at **Yieldingtree**, for this is another example of just

The Talbot at Chaddesley Corbett.

how easily corruptible minor place-names are. Historical records show this to be derived from '(place at) Gilda's tree', although the records do not show just when (or indeed why) the personal name was taken to be 'yielding'.

The **Talbot Inn** derives its name from the early variety of hound, the ancestor of the modern fox and stag hounds. Used for hunting and tracking, this white dog with black spots had long ears and heavy jaws, and had a remarkable ability to track its prey by scent alone. The pub name comes via the Talbot family, whose coat of arms includes a representation of the animal.

Chadwich

This is another place-name which has yet to be defined with any certainty. Listings such as *Celdvic* in 1086 and *Chadeleswik* in 1212 would suggest this is 'the farmstead of Ceadda'. Some maintain that the personal name here refers to St Chad, a bishop of Mercia who died in 672 after a life devoted to humility and piety. Yet the settlement pre-dates St Chad's life and thus cannot be named after the saint, although his name probably influenced the evolution of the place-name. Traditionally there was a church here dedicated to St Chad, which has been cited as the origin of the place-name. However this adds further weight to the earlier personal name of *Ceadda*, for canonisation does not occur until many years after the individual's death, thus the church cannot bear the name, and there is no reason for a church to be built without a community in residence from which to gather a congregation. The Chadwich estate was given to the National Trust by the Cadbury family.

The Salwarpe river rises at **Beacon Hill** (so-named as it was the site of a beacon signal fire), and is known as **Holywell** as it flows through Chadwich. The meaning of this river-name is not 'sacred water' as it would seem; the record of 1232 shows it to be a corruption of *Helliewell* which is 'a chalybeak spring', that is 'a stream impregnated with iron ore'.

Church Honeybourne and Cow Honeybourne

The two Honeybournes are very close together, standing alongside a stream east of Evesham referred to as *Hunigburna* in 1368, and separated by the old Roman road of Ryckneild Street. Predictably this is a 'stream on whose banks honey can be gathered'. Clearly it was necessary to differentiate between the two, the additions being self-explanatory.

Buckle Street is a portion of Icknield Street which passes Church Honeybourne. A charter of 709 names this as *Burghild's Street* which by 967 had become *Bucga's Street*. This does not represent a change of name, as Bucga is a short form of Bughild.

The name of **Poden** is derived from the name of a Saxon chieftain whose people resided at the settlement at 'Podda's hill'.

Church Lench

The Old English *hlenc* is a side form of *hlinc* which means 'hill' (*see* Ab Lench). The addition here is self-explanatory. Domesday records the place-name as *Circelenz*, and also imposed a tax on the orchards here, which would have made a small dent in the profits of the landholders at the church of Evesham.

Churchill (near Kidderminster)

Three early forms of this place-name, *Circhul* and *Cercehalle* in Domesday, and *Chyrchull* in 1275, would suggest the same meanings as the previous entry. There is a yew tree in the churchyard which would have been a sizeable tree by the time of the Domesday survey, when Walter was the man at the helm as the representative of William FitzAnsculf.

Old English *nemung* and Middle English *nimen* literally mean 'take by force'. As this is the origin of *Nemmings*, we can only assume the sense here is

All Saints' Church. Church Lench.

'reclaimed land' and refers to an overgrown area which was cleared from trees at a much earlier time.

The **Book and Candle** obviously derives its name from a religious reference, although whether this originated here, was transferred here by an earlier landlord or was simply selected from the list of names already in use, is not clear.

Churchill (near Worcester)

Only two early forms are found, *Circehille* from Domesday, and *Cherchhull* in 1209, literally 'church hill'. This could either refer to a hill with or near a church, or one belonging to a church. However, these early forms may be corrupted and the true origin could be a British hill-name *cruc*, to which was added the explanatory Old English *hyll*. If this is indeed the case, the name was mistakenly associated with the word church at a very early date.

Hops have long been an important crop in the county. It was inevitable that there would be a pub named the **Oast House**, a building specifically designed for drying the hops themselves.

Claines

The Saxon *claeg-naess* indicates this place north of Worcester originates in 'the clayey headland', further evidenced by the thirteenth-century listings as *Cleinesse* and *Cleines*.

To the trained eye the derivation of the name of **Astwood** here is clear: that this is the 'east wood' is confirmed by early Saxon forms. **Whistan** is from Saxon *hwit-stan*, named from a white stone erected here as a boundary marker and/or for some religious rite. During the time of William the Conqueror the stone was removed and used in building a privy for the monks of St Mary.

Unique in its location entirely within a graveyard, **The Mug House** is named from a seventeenth-century term for 'ale house' – mug being used in the sense 'pot' or 'ewer'.

Cleeve Prior

Early listings show the place once had the same name as its location: *Clive* and *Clyve* in Domesday, and *Clyve Prior* in 1291 all point to '(place at) the cliff or bank'. The distinctive addition comes from its early possession by Worcester Priory.

Two men dominate the history of Cleeve Prior, but for very different reasons. Its most famous son is Thomas Bushell (1599–1674), whose list of achievements is impressive. After negotiating the use of Welsh mines for the king and founding the mint in Aberystwyth, his career was interrupted by the Civil War when he fought on the side of the Royalists; indeed he led the final defence of Lundy Island. Following the victory by the Parliamentarians, he reopened both mines and mint in Cromwell's name. Bushell pioneered new techniques of adit mining, where the shaft enters horizontally rather than vertically. He was also highly knowledgeable in the refining of precious metals, making the discovery of a hoard of Roman gold coins here in 1811 something of a suspicious coincidence. Although he died in poverty, he left splendid aquatic gardens at **Enstone**.

Thirteenth-century politics being what they were, the notoriety achieved by William de Ledbury mirrors the man's lack of respect for authority on even the highest level. Evicted from Great Malvern in 1294, after conflicts with the Bishop of London, Edward I and even the Pope himself, he was given the face-saving appointment at Cleeve by the king (despite having already publicly renounced his faith). William de Ledbury was known to have had twenty mistresses, a number which was undoubtedly understated owing to his position in the church.

Clent

As with many places which take their names from hills and similar features, early forms are as the modern version. The name is an old word for 'a rocky hill', and is related to Old Swedish *klinter*, Old Norse *klettr*. Perhaps the original landlord was aware of this when he named the **Hill Tavern**. Oak Apple Day, the anniversary of the restoration of Charles II, is still marked in Clent south of Stourbridge today.

St Kenelm's Chapel is near a field called Cowbach, 'cow valley', which is traditionally held to be where the saint was murdered in 820.

The **Bell and Cross Inn** is hardly an exceptional name for a public house. There are many 'Bell' names throughout the land, many of which contain a second element as here. While the origins of this specific pub are unknown, many having simply taken established 'pub' names, and the general origins of the more common names are well known. In times when the vast majority never learned how to read, it made sense to dispense with a written form and to utilise pictorial representations. Signs could prove expensive if produced by skilled artists, so if working on a tight budget, landlords would enlist lesser talents and a bell was a relatively simple shape to produce. Often found close to a church, the Bell is often found with a second element such as Cross, Book, Candle which shows the religious connections. However, these secondary names are also known to have been added when a new landlord took up residence. Having previously served the public at the Cross, it is quite possible the new landlord added this to the earlier Bell when he moved in – like a hyphenated name on marriage.

The Fountain is a common pub name, which could have heraldic origins from the coat-of-arms of the local landowners, may be taken from the crest of either the Plumbers' Company or that of the Master Mariners, or may simply refer to a nearby spring or well.

Clifton-upon-Teme

Listed as *Cliftun* and *Cliftun ultra Tamedam* in 934, and *Clistune* in Domesday, this is 'the farmstead on a hill or a hill slope, found at the brink of a river' (for the river-name, *see* Teme).

The king's land here was administered by the Abbot of Cormeilles and Osbern FitzRichard, Robert d'Oilly acting as nominal tenant.

In 1270 Henry III recognised the importance of the place by granting Clifton a borough charter, along with a weekly market and an annual fair.

Local place-names are not what they first seem for the modern forms are major corruptions of the true name. These include **Ayngstree Farm**, which is derived from the Saxon term for the small farmstead which was here during their dominant period prior to the Norman Conquest. Early listings prove the origin has nothing to do with trees, this name is certainly '(place at) the steep hill track'.

Likewise **Hollands Mill** has nothing to do with the Netherlands, but is derived from 'Hud's bridge'. The person in question is hardly likely to have built the bridge, or even been primarily responsible for its construction. Said Hud would probably have simply lived in the cottage closest to the bridge, which would have been usable by foot passengers only.

Again **Mail Street** is another misnomer, for the name existed centuries before any regular postal service. The street-name is derived from an area here known to the Saxons as 'Maega's woodland clearing'.

Clopton

Found as *Cloptun* and *Cloptona* in the tenth and twelfth centuries respectively, the first element is an Old English *clop*, not recorded in independent use but found in such words as *clopaecer* and *clophyrst*, and related to Middle High German *klupf*, 'rock', or Middle Danish *klop*, 'block, lump'. Thus the name doubtless means 'the settlement at the hill'. Interestingly the same element is used elsewhere to refer to anything from a notable hill right down to the slightest rise of land.

Cofton Hackett

Found as *Coftune* in 780, *Coftun* in 849, and *Costone* in Domesday, this is 'the farmstead with a hut or shelter' from Old English *cofa-tun*. Urso d'Abitot, whose family name is found in place-names in the county, seized this manor north-west of Alvechurch from the Bishop of Worcester. Later ownership by William Haket and his family, who were here in 1166, led to the manorial addition. In 1633 Thomas Joliffe, a close friend of Charles I, took the manorial reins. Following the siege and capture of Hawkesley House, the king spent the night at Cofton Hall. Thomas Joliffe is known to have visited the fated monarch during his incarceration and accompanied him to the scaffold on the morning of his unjustified execution.

There are two place-names here, **Bittell Farm** and **Bittell Reservoirs**, the origins of which are uncertain. We do know that Emma Bytilde and Richard Bitild were living in neighbouring Alvechurch in 1275, although whether this tells us that the places took the family names or vice versa will probably remain unknown.

There is no doubt as to the origins of **Kettles Wood**. This is derived from a personal name Ketel, the family being here from at least 1271. Interestingly, this is one of the very few place-names of Worcestershire to show any Scandinavian influence, for while the name of Ketel would be expected in the north and east of England (the region known as *Danelaw* until England was united) the south and west remained under Saxon influence. This does not necessarily prove that Scandinavian families migrated following the Norman Conquest; more likely it suggests this was a Saxon family with a Scandinavian branch to their family tree.

Comberton

Situated 3 miles south-east of Pershore, the first element here is Saxon *Cumbria*, as seen in records as *Cumbrincgtun* in 972 and *Cumbrintune* in 1086, when it was under the control of Gilbert FitzThorol who is said to have collected great quantities of gold for the king. This element is used either as a personal name, possibly even a nickname, or a reference such as 'of Cumbrians'. The former is likelier as this name originates from 'the farmstead of the family or followers of Cumbra'; there is no reason to suspect Cumbrians ever migrated this far south owing to a lack of other examples.

Conderton

With records such as *Cantuaretun* in 875 and *Canterton* in 1201, this place south-east of Evesham has a name which is Old English *cantwaretun*, 'the farmstead of the Kentishmen'.

After the Roman departure in the middle of the fifth century, the peoples of the region roughly corresponding to modern Germany and Denmark were quick to expand their territories to encompass large stretches of England. Popularly known as the Anglo-Saxons, there were three distinct cultures: the Saxons, who dominated the lands across the Midlands, South and West; the Angles, who gave their name to the region where they settled, now known as East Anglia; and the Jutes, who limited their settlement areas to Kent and small parts of Sussex and Hampshire. The Jutes came from what is now Denmark. That they were decidedly different from the Angles and Saxons meant that their rare appearance outside the southeast, where they were dominant, is often reflected in the place-name – as is the case with Conderton.

Cook Hill

Another of Urso d'Abitot's holdings in the eleventh century, this name, unlike many hill names, has both elements of Saxon origin. The early records as *Cochilla* in 1156 and *Cochull* in 1262 show this is Old English *cocc-hyll*, literally 'hill hill'. However, the first element is also used to indicate the shape of the hill when used in such combinations such as this. Hence we can amend our definition to 'a heap' or perhaps 'hillock'. **Nunnery Wood** belonged to the nuns of Cook Hill from the twelfth century.

Cookley

Despite the similarity to both Cook Hill and Cooksey Green, the first element is not related to either. Indeed records such as *Culnan clif* in 964 and *Culla clife* in 1281 do not conclusively show the personal name here to be Culla, although it would certainly be related to the same (possibly a female version of that name). The modern name of Cookley would suggest the second element to be the Saxon *leah*, 'woodland clearing', whereas the true origin is *clif*, which is used to describe 'a slope, a cliff, or even a river-bank'.

Cooksey Green

This region of Upton Warren, the affix 'Green' being self-explanatory, tells us this was once 'Cucu's island, or dry land in a marsh'. This personal name seems to be a pet-form of many names which begin *Cwic-*, from Saxon *cwicu* meaning 'speedy, quick'. Early forms include *Cochesei* in Domesday, and *Cokeseya* in 1212. Domesday also records this as land held by Urso d'Abitot; here Herbrand and William took charge of daily affairs on his behalf.

Cotheridge

Records show *aet Coddan hrycce* in 963, *Coddan hrycge* in 1106, and *Codrie* in Domesday. This is undoubtedly 'Codda's ridge', a personal name found in many place-names but never found elsewhere. This may suggest that this is a nickname, perhaps for someone who administers or who works the land, performing a particular function in either case. The body of the church at Cotheridge, west of Worcester, is Norman, while parts of the timbered tower date from around 1300.

Cradley

The name of this place west of Malvern almost certainly originates from 'the wood and clearing of a man called Creoda', the common Saxon suffix *leah*, following the personal name. However, some point to the early forms such as *Cradeleie* in 1086 and *Ceadelega* in 1180 as evidence of an Old English word *cradol*, literally 'cradle' and used here in the sense of a hurdle or small fence. For many years this town on the outskirts of Stourbridge was famous for its gunsmiths.

Croome d'Abitot, Earls Croome, and Hill Croome

All three places were named from the local brook which flows past them and whose name was once undoubtedly Crombe, 'the winding stream'. Like many river and hill names, this has ancient origins in the British or Celtic languages spoken for centuries before the arrival of the Romans around the time of Christ's birth. The British *Cromba*, identical to the Welsh *crwm*, means 'crooked'. Another brook in Worcestershire is also referred to as *Crome* in 972, but even if it has managed to keep flowing as land drainage methods improved over the centuries, its whereabouts are as much of a mystery as the modern name.

Early forms of the place-names such as *Cromman, Cromban* in 969, and *Crumbe* in Domesday do not help us to recognise which of the three settlements is being spoken of. Yet it is clear from the later records of *Hylcromban* in 1038, *Crombe Dabetoth* in 1275, and *Erlescrombe* in 1495. Hill Croome stands predictably on the hill; Earls Croome was once under the control of the earls of Warwick; and the family name of d'Abitot is derived from Abbetot in France.

Croome Court and gardens had splendid beginnings, with Capability Brown, Adam and Chippendale all having a hand in its design.

The hamlet of **Boughton** near Hill Croome is derived from the Saxon *boc-tun*, 'the farmstead at or by the beech tree'.

Cropthorne

This place midway between Pershore and Evesham has records such as *Cropponthorn, Croppanthorn,* and *Cropetorn* found from the eighth, ninth and eleventh centuries respectively. At this time there was another settlement called *Croppedune,* now lost. This suggests that the first element is a hill-name Croppe, derived from *cropp.* The second element is Saxon *thorn* giving 'the thorn tree on or near a hill'. The church here has a Saxon cross.

Crowle

With records from the ninth century as *Crohlea,* and *Croelai* in Domesday, this place-name is derived from Old English *croh-leah,* 'the woodland clearing by the nook or corner of land'. At the end of the eleventh century Crowle had a working watermill and two salthouses.

Domesday also records a place named *Crull.* This is thought to have been named from a small stream, *Crulla, c.* 1100, whose name is derived from the Saxon *crull* meaning 'curly' and used here in the general sense 'winding'. Today no sign remains of the settlement or of the stream. Losing a stream is nothing remarkable: drainage systems increase the flow of water from the land and prevent it from filling the natural outlet which soon dries up and is reclaimed as agricultural land. Losing a settlement is quite possible, but usually some archaeological remnant is found, especially in the form of crop markings in aerial photographs. As no physical evidence of a lost settlement has been found, it may be that the 'lost' settlement was in fact Crowle.

D

Defford

With clear records as *Deopanforda* from 972 and *Depeford* in 1086, there can be no disputing this name is Saxon *deop-ford*, 'the deep ford'. The Saxons were soon replaced as landholders, for by the end of the eleventh century two immigrant Frenchmen held the reins on behalf of the church of Westminster.

Doddenham

Although similar to the following entry of Dodderhill, the origins are quite different. The eighth-century listing as *Dodhaema* and Domesday's *Dodeham* show the first element to be a personal name 'Dodda's homestead'. Gilbert FitzThorold held this hamlet at the end of the eleventh century.

The Defford Arms, the sign displaying the family coat-of-arms.

Dodderhill

Sounding similar to Doddenham but otherwise unrelated shows that it is important to gather as many early forms of a place-name as possible in order to define the name with confidence. *Dudrenhill* and *Duderhill* both date from the late twelfth century, pointing to 'the hill where dodder grew'. This parasitic vine of the genus *Cuscuta*, having slender, twining yellow or reddish stems with a few minute, scale-like leaves and whitish flowers is also found as *doder* in Middle Low German, and *dodra* in Swedish, while the Old Scandinavian form *dudra* is found in records dating from 1265.

The name of **Helpridge Farm** is descriptive, but hardly an accurate one. The literal meaning of '(place at) the excellent or useful ridge' offers no clue as to exactly what use the ridge was. However, archaeological evidence shows there used to be at least one watermill here, which could well mean the ridge provided not only a water supply, but formed a natural mill race to drive the machinery.

Dodford

The only early record we have is that of 1232 as *Doddeford*. This does not help as, without any comparisons, we have no way of knowing how accurate this record really is. However, there seem to be only two possibilities here: either the same (or similar) personal name to that found at Doddenham, hence 'Dodda's ford'; or less likely the same origin as Dodderhill, 'ford near where dodder is found'. The former definition is favoured as many river crossings were manned by those who collected tolls and maintained the crossing, while the plant dodder does not seem a suitable candidate for such a wet environment (although as a parasitic plant it is perfectly capable of adapting to a number of hosts with ease).

Dormston

The Domesday entry as *Dormestun* is clearly 'Deormod's farmstead'. However, there is an earlier form dating from 972 as *Deormodesealdtun* which gives a slightly different meaning of 'Deormod's old settlement'. This could simply be an example of how unreliable Domesday's forms may be, but with such an anomaly it is tempting to think that both forms may well be correct. Perhaps there were two settlements in the latter half of the tenth century, the original being abandoned by the time of the Domesday survey. Alternatively it could simply be that the inhabitants no longer referred to their settlement as 'old', and this was reflected in the place-name.

Doverdale

Domesday's entry as *Lunvredele* can be discounted as erroneous, and taking the 1166 record of Duverdale as a base, the settlement stood alongside what is now known as **Elmley Brook**, but before the twelfth century still retained its Old British or Celtic name which is still represented in the name of Doverdale. Hence from British *dubro* and Saxon *dael* this is '(the settlement on) water valley'. Traces of the old manor house moat are still visible around Doverdale Manor.

Draycott

The county has two places named Draycott, one near Blockley and another close to Kempsey. Listed as *Draicote* in 1209 and *Draycote* in 1275 respectively, they have identical meanings. From Old English *dragu-cot* this name is 'the cottages by a portage'. A portage refers to a stretch of land between two rivers across which boats were dragged to enable transfer from one river system to another; or sometimes an overland detour to avoid an impassable obstacle on the same river.

Droitwich

A variety of differing forms are found here: *Wiccium emptorium* in 716, *Saltwic* in 888, *Wich* in 1086, and *Drightwich* in 1347. The ninth-century record differs,

Droitwich's sign shows the town's historical importance as a source of salt.

This mural in the centre of Droitwich depicts several aspects of the town's history.

referring to Droitwich as 'Saltwich' (a remnant from the Roman name for this place of *Salinae*) and recalling the times when it was important for salt, a commodity used extensively to preserve meat.

From the other forms we see the place-name was originally simply Old English *wic*, used here in the sense of 'dwelling place'. The later addition of *dryht* or *drit* brings us to '(the dwelling place at) the dirty or muddy salt works'. The royal assent to produce salt at *Droitwaich* was granted by Edward III.

Found as *Wittona* in 716, *Wictun* in 817, and *Witone in Wich* in Domesday, derived from Saxon *wic-tun*, 'the farmstead by a wic' is today known as **Witton**, the *wic* in question being nearby Droitwich. The name of **Chauson** is a corrupt form of the Saxon *cealf-tun*, meaning 'farmstead where calves are kept'.

Probably best known for the imposing Chateau Impney, the name of **Impney** was originally 'Imma's island'. The second element here is Saxon *-eg*, literally 'island' but also used to refer to dry land surrounded (or almost) by a marsh or wetlands. A look at a contour map of this area makes it easy to see how there is a distinct rise here with low-lying land around.

Falsam Pits is a somewhat misleading name, for the affix did not appear until many years after 'Faele's homestead' had vanished leaving no trace of its early inhabitation (other than the place-name).

Much as the Hop Pole at Bromsgrove and the Ale Stake, the **Barley Mow** is a name which denotes the origins of the pub sign. The 'Mow' referred to the stack of

Chateau Impney, just outside Droitwich and now a hotel, was built in the 1870s by John Corbett, known as the 'Salt King'.

barley, a certain indication that beer was on sale. **The Castle** is one of those pub names which may have had obvious origins in being close to a castle, but was later utilised because: (i) it was a simple design for a sign; (ii) a reference to this element was featured in the landowner's coat of arms; or in more recent times, (iii) an allusion to 'an Englishman's home is his castle'. The sign of the **Old Cock** at Droitwich depicts a Silver Grey Dorking cockerel and notes 'the oldest English breed, dating from Roman times'. Be that as it may, the only reason this was chosen was for its use as a term of familiarity between friends since the eighteenth century. There is no reason to believe the **Rifleman's Arms** had any connection with gunsmiths (unless it was the former trade of an innkeeper here); it more plausibly refers to the user of the weapon, with the addition 'Arms' being a play on words. The **Ring o' Bells** is a common name, originally used to indicate a refreshment stop for local campanologists.

Dudley

Although now considered part of the West Midlands, Dudley was a part of Worcestershire for centuries and is still considered such by some who live there. With records such as *Dudelei* in 1086, *Duddele* in 1221, and *Doddeley* in 1279, there can be no doubt the name originated as 'the woodland clearing of Dodda'. Parts of the surviving castle are of Norman construction. The place is on the edge of the Black Country, so called because of stained brickwork from the smoke produced in the early days of the Industrial Revolution. Indeed, there is documented evidence that Dudley was using coal to smelt iron ore as early as the seventeenth century.

Netherton is as it sounds, 'the lower farmstead', the Saxon *nether* still in use in the sense 'lower'. **Ryall** comes from Old English *ryge-heale*, literally 'rye crops' and a reference to the speciality crop grown here. It is unusual to find a crop being grown singly prior to the Middle Ages; until then strip farming was the norm. Here one family would rent land from the landlord, growing as many different crops as they could to enable them to feed themselves. The amount of land rented depended on the size of the family, and the length of the strip. Payment was made to the landholder in the form of produce, a system which suited both parties. This agricultural system was in use for centuries, and survives in the regular corrugated effect still visible in those fields which have avoided modern ploughing machinery up to the present day. **Freebodies** is a region which takes its name from the tenants who were here from at least 1275, the Frebodi family.

Dunclent

Lying on the slope of the Clent Hills, the modern form is identical to that recorded in Domesday, and little different from the form dating from 1315 as *Dounclent*. The pronunciation of the fourteenth-century form is exactly what the name means, 'down (i.e. 'lower') Clent', describing this place's location perfectly. The Domesday landholder is given as St Guthlac's church, with the daily running of the holding left to a certain Nigel the Doctor.

Dunhampton

There are no early records of this place-name, only appearing as the modern version from 1222. Yet this is doubtless 'the hamtun on a hill'. Old English *hamtun* is a rare element found only in place-names, and used to denote 'the village proper'. From this we can deduce that the settlement had at least one (probably several) outlying minor settlements which were considered part of the whole and not named individually.

Some are of the opinion that *hamtun* points to the site of the chief manor of a large estate, where the smaller satellite dwellings were used by those who worked on the land in the name of the landlord. However, one would expect a man of such power and influence to have left his mark on the place-name itself, so perhaps this definition of *hamtun* is rather too fanciful.

E

Eardiston

With records from 957 as *Eardulfestun* and Domesday's *Ardolvestone*, this name comes from 'farmstead of a man called Eardwulf'. Another Domesday monastic holding, here of the church of Worcester, a fishery here produced food for their table and the pools also provided a food source for Knighton.

Eastbury

This small area by Hallow lacks a sufficient number of surviving early forms to enable us to define it with any certainty. However, it is quite possible that this settlement pre-dates its neighbour by several centuries. The Saxon *burg* almost always refers to a hill-fort, the fortified settlements inhabited since well before Roman times. Historical listings as *Earesbyrig* and *Eresbyrie* are insufficient to tie down the personal name with any degree of certainty, but it is probably something like 'Earnhere's defensive settlement'.

Eckington

Three early forms of this name: *Eccyncgtun* in 972, *Aichintune* in 1086, and *Akinton* in 1197, show how the modern name is closer (especially in pronunciation) to the earliest forms than to those found in the eleventh and twelfth centuries. This is rather unusual – normally the name continues to evolve away from the original rather than going back to its roots. Yet there is still some uncertainty as to the personal name on which the place-name is based. This is either 'the settlement of the family or followers of a man called Ecca', or perhaps his name was Ecci. Eckington is the site of one of the oldest bridges crossing the River Avon.

Eldersfield

As with Eckington, the early forms are insufficient to clarify the first element. Listed in 972 as *Yldresfeld*, in Domesday as *Edresfelle*, the 1156 record is as *Ederesfeld*, and forty years later as *Eldresfeld*. Some believe this to be a personal name, although there is even some disagreement as to whether the name is *Yldre*,

Eldre or *Ealdhere*. Yet there are also some who consider the *-d-* in the early forms to be an early intrusion, which would suggest the first element to be Saxon *ellern*. If this is the case then this is 'the open land where elder trees are found'. This would make more sense as the Saxon *feld* refers to a clearing and, although having the same uses as the modern field, would not have had a boundary fence or hedge. Hence any elder trees could have formed a natural boundary, this for identification purposes and not solely to provide a barrier to prevent livestock from straying.

Domesday records that Eldersfield was held by Reinbald the Chancellor prior to the Norman Conquest. Also known as Reinbald the priest, he was appointed first Chancellor of England by Edward the Confessor in 1042. Much of the surviving church here is of Norman design, within which the coat of arms of Dick Whittington's family is displayed.

Two minor place-names here are worth noting. The strangely named **Corse Lawn** suggests one meaning today, yet the origins are quite different. Worcestershire was once even closer to the Welsh border and this name is derived from a form of the Welsh *cors* meaning 'a marsh'. In later years the affix was used to denote a grassy area as drainage improved.

There is also the name of **Drinkers End**. It is easy to see how the family name of le Drynkar, who were here in 1297, has remained virtually unchanged over seven centuries. The additional 'end' first appears during the seventeenth century, used here in the sense of 'a place'.

Elmbridge

For once Domesday's *Elmerige* is much closer to the modern name than that found in 1287 as *Ammerugge*, even if it does erroneously suggest a bridge. The true derivation is Old English *elmen-ric*, literally 'ridge of elm trees'.

Nearby stands Purshall Court, which was used on several occasions by the conspirators in the Gunpowder Plot.

Elmley Castle

Found as *Elmlege* in 780, *Elmelege* in 1179, *Elmeleye* in 1312, and *Elmeleye Castel* in 1327, this settlement was found in or near 'the woodland clearing among the elm trees'. The affix, first seen in the fourteenth century, refers to the castle which once stood here.

The names of two places here, **Cames Coomb Fields** and **Cames Wood**, predictably share a common origin. Both were named after the Caan family who lived in adjoining Great Comerton and either lived or worked here at some time. There is documented evidence of John Caan living in the neighbouring village in 1327.

The **Queen Elizabeth Inn** is one of literally hundreds of pubs showing allegiance to the monarch, past or present. Interestingly the popularity of 'monarch' names rose with the dissolution of the monasteries by Henry VIII, mainly because innkeepers were reluctant to incur the wrath of the king and changed their sign from a papal image to that of royalty. Later the removal of Charles I from the throne had the reverse effect, only to see an increase in numbers again following the Restoration.

Elmley Lovett

Listings such as *Elmesetene gemaere* in 817, *Aelmeliea* in Domesday, *Almeleye Lovet* in 1275, and *Elmeleye Lovet* in 1285 confirm this has the same origin as Elmley Castle as 'the woodland clearing among the elm trees'. Here the distinguishing manorial addition is that of the Lovett family, an Old French byname which became a family name and meant 'wolf cub'; the Lovetts were here by the thirteenth century.

Prior to the Norman Conquest Elmley Lovett was held by Queen Edith, daughter of Earl Godwin and Edward the Confessor's queen. This holding must have been a prosperous one, for it boasted three watermills and four salthouses.

St Michael and All Angels' Church at Elmley Lovett.

Domesday often records holdings as simply 'king's land' which applies both to before and after the Conquest. Although these would have officially been held by King Harold until he lost his throne to William I in 1066, Domesday's references are to his predecessor, Edward the Confessor. The Normans did not recognise Harold's claim to the throne, and therefore he is not credited in Domesday.

Here we find **Pepwell Farm**, known to the Saxons as '(the place at) Pyppa's spring', a name which originally applied to the spring and was applied to the small farmstead which grew because of the reliable water source.

Nearby is **Whitlinge** which is certainly derived from the Old English meaning 'white ridge'. Today it is hard to see just why this region was considered 'white'; possibly the sense here is 'bright' if the surrounding woodland meant the land around here was particularly well shaded. Certainly there is no reason to believe the soil exhibited any chalky characteristics, as is often the case with such names.

Evesham

Two records dating from 817 refer to this settlement as simply *Homme* and also as *Eveshomme*. By 1017 we find *Eoueshamme*, while the Domesday entry is exactly as it appears in the modern form. The second element is from the Saxon word *hamm*, used to describe a water meadow or land alongside a meandering stream. Hence the origins here are '(place at) the land in the river bend of a man called Eof'.

The site of the former Evesham Abbey, now home to two churches and a sixteenth-century bell tower.

Dating from 1400, the Almonry now houses Evesham's museum and tourist information office.

Bengeworth is a hamlet near Evesham which is derived from the Old English for 'the enclosed settlement of the family or followers of Benna'. By the eleventh century this was part of the extensive lands of the Abbot of Evesham and Urso the Sheriff representing Worcester Church.

Pubs which have the name **Bear** are normally prefixed by a colour, which is indicative of heraldic origins. Older premises (without assigned colours) almost certainly refer to the sport of bear-baiting, which was finally made illegal in 1835. Many signs were altered after this barbaric sport was banned, for obvious reasons.

Created in the early nineteenth century, the **Oddfellows Arms** were so-named to indicate the Independent Order of Oddfellows who met within. Their name is said to have come following some off-the-cuff remark made about the founding members.

F

Fairfield

Appearing as *Forfeld* in 817, the name had changed little by 1255 when recorded as *Forfeud*. While the modern name suggests a pleasant and attractive clearing, this seems unlikely as the true origin is Saxon *for-*, literally 'at the front', and *-feld*, 'open country'. Written evidence shows a fortified mansion with a defensive moat was erected here known as Fairfield Court and, together with the open country, the estate encompassed woodland extending over 5 miles in length. This place is thought to have been of some significance in the late Saxon era; indeed there is reason to believe this was the site of a court house for prison records show offenders sentenced to anything from incarceration to the gallows were tried around here. The manor was returned to Worcester Cathedral in 1057 on the orders of Lady Godgifu (Godiva), her husband Leofric having had a long-standing argument with this particular church leading to some damage of the monastic holdings.

Together with a passing reference to the majestic bird itself, the **Swan Inn** took its name from the coat of arms of a family who were prominent in this region.

Feckenham

If we dismiss Domesday's *Fecheham* as the best phonetic version the Norman surveyors could muster, then the records from 804 and 960 as *Feccanhom* and *Feccanham* seem fairly straightforward. However '(place at) the water meadow belonging to Fecca' provides us with a dilemma, for such a personal name is not recorded elsewhere. There is evidence of Facca as a personal name, but these records are few and far between and can hardly be considered as relevant to Feckenham. Undoubtedly this is a personal name (possibly a nickname) but will probably remain unknown.

The Norman landholder, William FitzOsbern, palatine of Hereford and confidant of William I, had transferred Feckenham to Herefordshire, despite it being far removed from the borders. Much of Herefordshire was laid waste at this time, the principal reason being the incursions of one Edric the Wild, whose followers were to prove a nuisance in the western marches for many years. Yet this change of county was only on paper, being chosen because of the long-standing strength of the local economy.

Feckenham Forest once covered a large area, and was a major contributor to the district's wealth. Gradually the great forest dwindled, comparatively little being left by 1389 when Geoffrey Chaucer held the posts of Clerk of Works and Keeper of the Lodge. History records numerous physical confrontations between those who cared more for the timber potential (the landholders) than they who relied on it on a daily basis for their domestic needs (the commoners). In 1558 Sir John Throckmorton, then lord of the manor, was left homeless when an angry mob tore his house down. Hardly a tree survives today, although the network of bridle paths which are still marked on maps do show where the heart of the ancient forest stood untouched for centuries.

The region known as **Shurnock** derives its name from the Old English for 'white-leaved, bright, even brilliant oak'. For the name to have endured, the tree in question, or its leaves, must have been exceptionally light in colour. Furthermore the oak would have had some significance, possibly as a boundary marker and/or the site of a religious rite.

Some believe the Domesday entry of *Swinehel* to be an early form of **Shepley**. However, this eleventh-century entry is probably a lost settlement, and the name has nothing to do with 'swine'. Indeed there are examples of Shepley the length and breadth of England, every one of which is derived from Old English *sceap-leah*, 'woodland clearing where sheep are pastured', which is confirmed by the record of 1272 as *Shepeley*. There is no argument with the unusual name of **Sillins** either, for early forms conclusively prove this is simply the quite common reference to 'plough land', although having almost unique modern form.

Twatling Road is often found for side branches off Roman roads. The Upper Saltway crosses Lickey Hill and Twatling Road connected this track with Icknield Street. The etymology of the name is obscure, although it has been suggested that the name has been borrowed from Watling Street; this seems most unlikely, especially considering there are a number of examples and very few are not connected to this major Roman road.

Fladbury

Fladbury, 'stronghold or manor house of a woman called Flaede', is seen in records such as *Fledanburg* in 692, *Flaedanbyrg* in 778, and Domesday's *Fledebirie*. The name is a short form of many names including Aethelflaed.

The name of **Craycomb**, existing as a road name and in fields, is derived from the Saxon for 'valley where crows are seen'.

The **Anchor Inn** would seem to be associated with the sea, and indeed a former mariner may well have 'dropped anchor' at Fladbury after ending his career on the high seas. However, the name also has religious connections: the words of St Paul – 'a steadfast anchor of the soul, a hope' (Hebrews 6:19) – are self-explanatory.

The delightful sign at Fladbury . . .   *. . . and its reverse.*

However the earliest names would more likely have referred to anker, a measurement approximately equivalent to 8½ gallons, especially when these places brewed their own ales. It should also be noted that the name may have no relevant basis, other than being a relatively simple image to create on the sign.

The **Chequers Inn** is a very old name first brought to this country by the Romans, and evidence from the ruins of Pompeii suggest the sign was used long before. Originally the chequerboard, or a representation, would have been hung outside to indicate a game similar to draughts was played within. Later the same sign was associated with a money-table and gave rise to 'exchequer', itself once used to refer to a chessboard. It is easy to see how the sign quickly became a pointer to a changer of money or banker of some description.

Flyford Flavell

Early records of this name are plentiful: *Fleferth* in 930, *Flaeferth* in the mid-tenth century, *Flefero* in 972, *aet Fleferht* in 1002, *Flavel* in 1212, and *Flefrith* in 1317.

However, despite these many forms the name is still difficult to tie down with any degree of certainty. The name of Flyford has nothing to do with a river crossing, the Old English element here is not *ford* but *fyrhth*, meaning 'sparse woodland'. The first element may be a personal name, but this seems unlikely. There are some who would argue that Flyford was previously known as *Aelflaedetun*, or more likely a place in Flyford was known by the name. A shortened version of this or a similar name (as noted under the entry for Fladbury) may be the first element here.

It should be noted that the majority of the Saxon forms come from transcripts dating from around 1500. By this time the native language had evolved to Middle English which, although not dissimilar to its predecessor, was sufficiently different to have made it easy for errors to have crept into the transcripts.

The addition of Flavell does not have manorial origins; indeed it is simply a Normanized form of Flyford, added to distinguish this place from Grafton Flyford.

Fosse Way

This well-known Roman road running from Exeter to Lincoln has a very un-Roman sounding name, not that the Romans were a leading light in creating place-names; indeed they were content to 'Latinise' existing names. The name refers to the construction of the Roman roads and to the drainage ditches running along both sides. Hence this can hardly have been the Roman name (which is unknown), but is derived from Old English *foss* meaning 'ditch'.

Franche

Although the only early form of this name found is as *Frenesse* in Domesday, there can be no doubt that this is '(place at) the ash tree of a man called Frea', the Saxon personal name being combined with Old English *aesc*.

Frankley

While early records are sparse, this place-name comes from the Saxon '(place at) the woodland clearing of a man called Franca'. Domesday tells us the village of *Franchelie* was maintained by one Baldwin on behalf of William FitzAnsculf. Also known as William of Pinkeni, hailing from Picquigny, Somme in France, his standing among the hierarchy of the land was assured as the son of the Sheriff of Buckinghamshire. William had his seat at Dudley Castle.

G

Grafton Flyford

The additional Flyford did not appear before the sixteenth century (*see* Flyford Flavell).

The name of Grafton appears as *Graftun* in 884 and *Garstune* in Domesday. Clearly the Domesday entry is in error and this originates from Saxon *graf-tun*, 'the settlement in or by a grove'. Grafton Manor has identical origins, recorded as *Grastone* in 1086 and *Grafton* in 1212, while the additional Manor is self-explanatory.

The oddly named **Libbery** literally means 'projecting earthwork'. From this we can safely assume it to have been an unusual or greatly pronounced projection, for by definition any such construction displays such characteristics.

Greenhill

Although the images conjured up by the names of Greenhill and Grimley are very different, the origins of the first element are identical. Listed as *Grimeshyll* in 816, *Grimanhyll* in 957, and *Gremanhil* in Domesday, the name originates from the Old English *grima-hyll* '(place at) the hill of the ghost or spectre'. The term *grima* is not used in a literal sense here, but is a Scandinavian personal name, Grima, derived from the same origins.

Grimley

Listed as *Grimanlea*, *Grimanleage* and *Grimanleh* in the ninth and eleventh centuries, the first element of this place-name is identical to its near neighbour of Greenhill and is discussed under that entry. The suffix here is from Saxon *leah*, '(place at) the woodland clearing'.

After his capture by the British in 1810, Lucien, a brother of Napoleon Bonaparte, lived in Grimley for a number of years.

The name of **Monkwood** is of obvious derivation. Suffice to say this place was among the holdings of the monastery at Worcester.

H

Habberley

Recorded as *Harburgelei* in Domesday, and *Harberlega* in 1184, there is some doubt as to the correct personal name featured here. This is either 'settlement at the woodland clearing of a woman called Heathuburg', or it may be another female personal name, Heahburg.

Hadzor

With only two early forms available, *Headdesofre* and *Hadesore*, the name seems to derive from '(place at) the ridge of a man called Headd'. While the personal name is certain, it seems unlikely that the settlement would have been built on the top of the ridge. The name is probably misleading and should point to the settlement on the slope below the ridge.

Occasionally we find names which paint a picture of life during Saxon times. This is because some Saxon phrases relate to a very specific item or function. An excellent example of such is found in **Cockshull Hill**. This name is found throughout the land, in a variety of spellings and endings (Cockshot being the most common). Clearly a reliable water source was a major priority when selecting a site for settlement; however, even the smallest geological change can divert a watercourse or, more commonly, introduce impurities into the water. To find another water supply, even if it meant transporting the water, was preferable to relocating the settlement. This name reveals the ingenuity of these people in 'a spring or rivulet on a bank or slope to which a trough or spout was fixed to allow water to be collected and transported for domestic use'. While such a lengthy definition may seem improbable (especially for a comparatively short place-name), the complexities of the Germanic language group reveal this to be the case (along with prior knowledge of how these people lived). Note the water is deemed for 'domestic use', which is further evidence that the original water supply had become polluted in some way, but was still used by livestock and to irrigate crops when necessary.

Huntingtrap Farm is the only surviving remnant of a small hamlet which was initially 'the hunting village'. Records show this land was then in the hands of Dodford Priory, in which case they probably allowed hunting to take place here in lieu of tax payments.

Hagley

The only form available to us is Domesday's *Hageleia*. However, this is enough for us to be fairly certain of the origins. The first element is not a personal name, as may at first be suspected, but the Saxon *hag*, 'haws'; hence, '(the place at) the woodland clearing where haws, the fruit of the hawthorn, are found'. That the hawthorn is widely distributed over the whole of the country makes it surprising that this element is not found more often in place-names. **Hagley Hall** is still a quite splendid Palladian mansion, exhibiting some of the finest examples of eighteenth-century paintings and furniture.

Nearby **Harberrow** is another place-name of Saxon origin. Here we find the '(place at) the herdsman's hill', from Old English *hierdan-beorge*.

Halesowen

The earliest forms of *Hala* in 1086 and *Hales* in 1195 show the name was originally taken from the Old English plural of *halh* meaning 'a corner of land'. This was a general term used to refer to a recess or valley in a hill.

The second element is not seen before 1276 when Halesowen is referred to as *Hales Ouweyn*. This is undoubtedly a reference to Owen, son of David, a Welsh prince who married a sister of Henry II. He was made Lord of Hales in 1204.

The church at Halesowen has retained some of its original Norman architecture, and stands on the site of the earlier wooden Saxon church.

The region of Halesowen known as **Hill** is self-explanatory, coming from the Saxon word *hyll*. The Germanic language group, of which Saxon or Old English is an example, has also influenced place-names on continental Europe. **The Hawn**, which is from the Saxon *hagan*, meaning 'enclosed or fenced-in place,' comes from the same root as the basis for The Hague in the Netherlands.

Langley is a common place-name throughout England, usually found with a distinguishing second element. This part of Halesowen has always been known simply as Langley, which is always 'the long woodland clearing', a reference to its shape.

Hallow

From the ninth century we find records of *Halheogan*, *Heallingan*, and *Hallege*. All these point to an origin in the Saxon *hagan-halh*, 'enclosures in a nook or corner of land': an apt name for a place which lies in a tongue of land between two streams.

Moseley is a common minor place-name found all over England. It comes from the Saxon *musleage*, meaning 'woodland clearing infested by mice'.

Presumably the mice would have proliferated, having fed on the grain stores of the settlement; so before the people arrived, the population of rodents would have been kept in check by the amount of food available. The name of **Peachley** is, predictably, a reference to the peach. However, the derivation is not directly from the fruit or the tree on which it grows. This land was once held by the Peche family, itself taken from the Old French word for 'peach'. The second element of the place-name makes this '(place at) the woodland glade of the Peche family'.

Hampton

Not the same origins as Hampton Lovett, *Hamtone* in 709, *aet Heantune* in 780, *Heamtun* and *Hamtun* in the tenth century, and *Hantun* in Domesday show this is from Old English *hea-tun*, 'the high farmstead'.

Hampton Lovett

The first word is a very common place-name, having three different origins. Here it is from the Saxon *ham-tun*, suggesting 'home farm, homestead,' and appeared as *Hamtona* in 716, *Hamtune* in Domesday, and as *Hamton Lovet* in 1291, which is remarkably close to the modern form considering it was noted more than seven centuries ago. As expected, the addition comes from the manorial lords of the thirteenth century, the Luvet family. Lovett is from Old French *lovet*, meaning 'wolf cub', and would have been used as a nickname originally.

Nearby **Crutch Hill** is derived from the Middle English *cruche*, 'cross', referring to a wayside cross erected near here by nuns. **Fibden Farm** is named from the Saxon describing '(the place at) Febba's settlement on a slope'.

Hanbury

There is the same first element here as is found in Hampton, but which may have a slightly different meaning. From Old English *hean-burg*, this is 'the high fortified place', where 'high' is possibly used as a statement of rank rather than altitude. It is found as *Heanburh* in the eighth century, *Heanbyrg* in 836, and as *Hambyrie* in Domesday.

There is no more popular pub name in the land than that of the **Red Lion**, with almost seven hundred examples to date. As with all colour/animal names, this is of heraldic derivation. However, the pub name and the symbolic representation are so popular, it is impossible to know the origins. What is certain

This is the view across the Warwickshire/Worcestershire border from Hanbury Church. The plinth and panoramic map were erected to celebrate the new millennium.

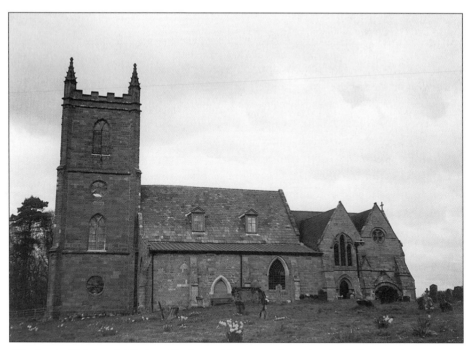

The church of St Mary the Virgin at Hanbury, with a carpet of snowdrops in the foreground.

is that the red lion represented John of Gaunt, the most powerful man in England in the fourteenth century, and is also synonymous with Scotland.

While *Loggerheads* has come to mean 'two or more parties in disagreement', as a place-name it has a totally different meaning. The word is a term found only in the Midlands for knapweed, *Centaurea nigra*, which flourishes here. The plant has purple thistle-like flowers and had some uses as a herb.

Hanley Castle, Child and William

The three Hanleys have the same origins, for the basic name is Saxon *hea-leah* '(place at) the high woodland clearing', as seen *Hanlege, Heanlega, Hanleg, Chuldrenehanle*, and *Williames Henle* in records dating from Domesday until 1275.

Hanley Castle was obviously the site of a castle, and traces of the castle moat are still visible today. Hanley Child represents the Saxon word *cilda*, meaning literally 'children', and is used here in the sense of 'noble born son', unlikely to have been of true noble birth but probably born into the family of a high-ranking churchman. Hanley William was either named from William de la Mare who held the manor in 1212, or it may have been the William de la Mare whose son is known to have held this place in 1198.

Hartlebury

Heortlabyrig in 817, *Heortlanbyrig* in 1320, and *Huerteberie* in Domesday all point to the origins being 'the strongholding of a man called Heortla'. The same man is also represented by the record of *Heortlaford* in 985, a place which lies within the bounds of Hartlebury. The castle at Hartlebury belonged to the Bishops of Worcester from the thirteenth century.

From the Saxon *lin-cumb* comes the name of **Lincomb**, 'the valley where flax grows (or possibly is grown)'. The name of **Shenstone**, which is found several times in the Midlands, denotes '(place by) the beautiful or shining stone'. The stone in question was almost certainly a boundary marker, although if the stone had been of suitable size and shape it would also probably have been a place of worship – in both Christian times and previously.

Harvington

Harvington lies adjacent to Chaddesley Corbett. There are two schools of thought regarding the derivation of its name. Some maintain it is a personal name coming

Harvington Hall.

from 'the farmstead of a woman called Herewynn', and pointing to the record of 1275 as Herewinton as evidence. However, to give a meaning from just one form often gives misleading results, especially when that single record is so long after the Saxon domination of the county had ended. Defining place-names is not an exact science, and much is open to interpretation by the individual. And while the evidence for Old English *here-ford-tun* is not much stronger, the eighth-century record of *Herverton* together with *Herferthun* in Domesday seems to mean 'farmstead near the ford suitable for the passage of an army' is probably at the very least closer to true origins.

Hatfield

From Old English *haethfeld*, this name refers to the '(place at) the feld or open land where heather and similar shrubs grow'. This is seen in the record of 1275 as *Hathfeld*, and in that of 892 as *Australis Hethfeld*. The additional 'Australis' in the late ninth century simply means 'southern'.

A tasteful modern road sign.

Heightington

Despite the reasonably late records of 1275 and 1332 as *Hutinton* and *Hutdynton* respectively, there can be no doubt this is 'the farmstead of the family or followers of Hyht'.

Henwick

Only two forms have ever been found of this place-name, *Higna gemaere* in 851 and *Henewic* in 1182. These two forms show the origin to be Old English *higna-wic*, 'the specialised farm of the religious people', to give it its most general definition. However, it is fairly safe to assume this referred to monks, or to those who worked the land on their behalf, and that it was almost certainly a dairy farm.

Hill and Moor

It hardly seems worthwhile listing this place in order to define such an obvious name, other than to note that it was simply known as *Hylle* in 1050, but by the time of Domesday thirty-six years later had become *More et Hylle*. That the name itself is unremarkable (or should that be names?) is a curiosity in that only a handful of unembellished hills and moors exist anywhere in England. Most have managed to be adorned by the name of someone or something in order to give them some degree of originality. Perhaps that these were unknown beyond the local community meant there was never any reference to them other than by the locals as simply 'the hill' and 'the moor'.

Himbleton

Appearing as *Hymeltun* in 816, this has its origins in Saxon *hymele-tun*, 'farmstead where hymele grows'. *Hymele* is a term which may refer to a number of plants, but it is quite likely used here to mean hops. If this is indeed the case, then there is a written record on the maps of the county which shows that hops were grown here at least twelve hundred years ago, a tradition which lives on today and will continue to do so.

Much as it seems pointless including a place-name for which there is no known definition, especially one as small as **Fepston**, it does include a unique element and thus is worthy of inclusion. Early forms are limited and of little assistance for they are all similar to the modern form. There is no other place in England that we could find beginning with *Fep-* or *Phep-* (and in any case, 'ph' is not found in Old English, the source language implied by the suffix -tun), which would suggest it is either a corrupted name which has stuck, or an unknown personal name.

By contrast, **Foredraught Lane** is found all over England as the name of tracks, lanes and pathways. Furthermore, it is always used to specifically describe a path from a farm to a main road used for the transportation of produce and/or supplies.

Hindlip

This is an interesting name which does have a connection with deer as it suggests. The tenth-century record of *Hindehlep* is clearly Old English *hinde-hliep*, 'a leap-gate for hinds'. It was desirable to include a deer-leap in the enclosures used for grazing the farmstead's livestock, easily achieved by simply making the fence a little lower in just one place. Having cleared the area to be set aside for pasture, it was just as desirable for the wild animals as it would have been to the domesticated creatures. To have built the fence higher all around would not have been a great deterrent for the deer, and would probably have resulted in the fence being damaged as they sought to gain entry. Hence to offer them the opportunity to browse when the livestock were securely locked up for the night would keep fence maintenance to a minimum, and would have had little effect on the grazing for their animals.

The present manor house dates from the nineteenth century. Earlier buildings on this site hosted meetings of the conspirators of the Gunpowder Plot, and earlier of those who planned to put Mary Stuart on the English throne, in the so-called Babbington Plot. Whether such a sordid past influenced the decision to rebuild on this site is not recorded.

Holdfast

Another place-name which has defied the best attempts to tie down its origins. Listed as *aet Holenfesten, aet Holanfaestene*, and *Holefaest* in the tenth and eleventh centuries, there can be no doubt the second element is Old English *faesten*, 'a stronghold'. That is preceded by something which looks very much like a form of Saxon *holh* meaning 'hollow', but this does not result in a plausible meaning. The likelihood is that it comes from *holegn*, referring to 'holly', although it is possibly a personal name, Hola, which is related to Old High German Huolo, found as a common element in place-names in and around Germany.

Holt

A very common element in place-names, Old English *holt*, meaning 'wood', is usually found as a second element preceded by the name of the tree that either dominated the region by numbers, or was the most sought after as a resource.

The farms near Holt still recall a former watermill which stood on **Grimley Brook**. Until the eleventh century the stream was known as *Baele*, from the Saxon *bael*, meaning 'fireplace', 'hearth', or even 'funeral pyre'. Today this name is remembered as **Ball Mill**. This unusual, and seemingly inappropriate, derivation could be explained by the archaeological evidence of iron smelting nearby.

Hopwood

Recorded as *Hopwuda, Hopwudeswic* and *Hopwuda* in the eighth and ninth centuries, this would appear to be a common Saxon place-name element, *hop*, meaning 'valley'. However, unless there has been an unprecedented movement of the land and the supposed valley has disappeared, this cannot be the origin of Hopwood. There is a similar word *hopu*, meaning 'privet', which may well be the origin here – but we can never know if this is truly 'the privet wood'.

Huddington

Hudigtuna gemaera in 840 and Domesday's *Hundintune* clearly give this place-name as meaning 'the farmstead of the family or followers of a man called Huda'.

An ancient cruck cottage at Huddington.

Huddington Court was named as the headquarters of those who conspired to blow up the Houses of Parliament in what was to become known as the Gunpowder Plot.

Hunnington

Although a very similar name to Huddington, this does not have a personal name as the first element. Here the origins are Saxon *hunig-tun*, 'the farmstead where honey was produced'. Honey was not only a valuable commodity as a food source, but was also used to settle dues to the lord of the manor in the form of rent and/or taxation, trade being much preferred by the poorer folk as they had little use for money, being unable to count.

Many minor place-names can be very specific, giving us a clue as to the uses of such sites prior to the Norman Conquest. **The Breach** is one such place, for it describes 'land broken by the plough', not particularly informative on its own but offering up more information when compared to land around here (i.e. not ploughed, hence used as pasture, which in turn gives an indication of the number of domestic animals kept and the number of people supported by the area of land set aside for cultivation).

Icknield Street

This ancient trackway is also known as **Ryknild Street** and runs from Bourton-on-the-Water in Gloucestershire to Rotherham in Yorkshire. Many feel this to have originally been a similar name to that of the Icknield Way, which runs from Dorset to Norfolk, and has become corrupted over the centuries to have an identical name today. The record of *Icenhylte* in 903 is of little help, as this was doubtless influenced by the name of the Hwiccan tribesfolk who were in residence around this quarter of England. Furthermore it has been suggested that Hwiccan is the origin of the name, but this is not possible. The Hwiccan did not arrive in England prior to the departure of the Romans in 453, and by the fifth century this trackway was already ancient (certainly pre-dating Roman Britain by several hundred years).

Unless a very early form of this track-name is uncovered, it seems the meaning will always remain a mystery.

The Bull's Head Inn, Inkberrow.

The Old Bull at Inkberrow.

Inkberrow

Just how or when the personal name Inta was corrupted to become Ink- is a mystery. Indeed, we would expect the '-t-' to have been retained and the loss of the '-b-'. However, *Intanbeorgas* in 789, *Intanbeorgum* in 822, and *Inteberge* in 1086 is certainly '(place at) the hills or mounds of a man called Inta'. It is tempting to think these mounds were man-made, possibly tumuli or burial-mounds, but no archaeological evidence has been found to substantiate this. Charles I spent the night before the Battle of Naseby in 1645 at Inkberrow, leaving a book of maps behind him when he left the next morning.

An interesting place-name is found near Inkberrow. It is unusual in that it has none of the common elements found in place-names, and does not feature a personal name. Indeed, the definition means that **Bouts** is one of those places which tells us something about the place as it was when the settlement was first established. The origin is a Saxon word which spoke of a measure of land. The actual area could vary to some degree, because it was not measured using standardised units. The derivation here is from 'the amount of ground covered by a furrow and back when ploughing or sowing', which could differ depending on the soil, the ploughman or his team of oxen. However, it does tell us that this was a very small place, only large enough to support a small family (or even an individual).

Another name of interest to toponomists is that of **Cank**, a former enclosure in **Nunnery Wood** which has left its mark on the landscape. This is a Midland dialect word used to describe a vocal sound as in 'chatter, gabble, cackle', and most often applied to geese. Yet if geese were the subject, we would expect these birds to be featured in the place-name at some stage (which they are not). Therefore it seems that in this instance the term is used as a derogatory one to refer to a former resident.

Of more traditional derivation is **Cladswall**. Featuring the Saxon element *hale*, this is 'Clodd's meadow land'. Old English also provided us with the definition of 'Ecga's oak', although without the series of early forms, this could hardly be seen from the modern place-name of **Edgiock**.

'A bird in the hand is worth two in the bush' is an extremely ancient proverb. **The Bird In Hand** at Inkberrow has the same meaning, and has been popular as a pub name since the seventeenth century. The name of the **Red Hart Inn** refers to the male red deer; whether this was a particularly impressive stag which was often seen around here, or perhaps the victim of a famous hunt, is not known.

Isbourne, River

Although this river could hardly be considered a major waterway, it must have been called something by those who lived near here on and off for centuries prior to the arrival of the Romans at around the time of Christ. Yet whatever the British name was, this is now lost. What remains is the Saxon name, clearly a back-formation from the settlement here. Recorded as *Esenburnen* in 709, *Esegburna* in 777, *Esingburnan* in 930, and *Eseburne* in 988, this is 'the stream (by the place) of the family or followers of Esa'.

Ismere

Unlike Isbourne, Ismere contains a river-name regarding which we are well aware of very ancient forms. Listed as *Husmerne* in 736, *Usmerorum* in 757, and *Usmere* in 964, the second element here is Saxon *mere*, 'lake'. The first element is a corrupted version of the element found in such river-names as Ouse, probably referring to the name of the stream which runs through (and indeed forms) the lake itself.

Ouse is a British river-name derived from an ancient root *ved-* or *ud-* meaning 'water'. Similarly we find the Sanskrit *udan*, 'water', and *udra*, 'a water animal', (which is the origin of 'otter'), and Old Irish *usce* which is also simply 'water'. The ancient root of *ud-* evolved through *udso*, *usso*, *uss*, and *us* to Old English *use*. The true base to the English river-names is *udsa*, a very ancient word found throughout the Indo-Germanic family of languages meaning 'well'.

The early forms include *Usemerorum*, a Latin form of a tribal name *Usmere* meaning 'the people at Usmere' and showing the early name of the stream.

K

Kempsey

Over a period of 300 years from the end of the eighth century this place is listed as *Kemesei*, *Cymesig*, *Kymesei*, *Kemesige* and *Chemesege*, which is clearly 'Cymi's island'. Island here is used in the sense of dry land in marshy ground, as there is no reason to believe it was ever entirely surrounded by water.

Henry III is said to have heard mass here, with his captor Simon de Montfort, before the Battle of Evesham in 1265; while the **Ketch Inn** reputedly played host to Samuel Butler for at least part of the time when he was writing *Hudibras*, published in 1663.

There is a hill near Kempsey known as **Bannutt Hill**. While the same element is seen near Bewdley Chaseleye in **Bannutt Tree Farm**, these are the only three examples of this name found. This suggested a personal name but, on investigation, was found to be a local dialect word used to refer to the walnut tree and to its fruit. The etymology of bannutt is unknown, although it probably used to mean 'bone nut' or 'nut with a bone-like shell'.

Converted oasthouses at Kempsey.

With its origins in Old English, the Saxon hamlet of **Kersewell** is from 'the spring where watercress grows'. **Napleton**, too, is Old English from 'the settlement at or by the orchard'.

Kenswick

Despite the record of *Checinwiche* in Domesday being markedly different from the thirteenth-century listings as *Kekingwik* and *Kekingewic*, there can be no doubting the personal name here. This is 'the wic of the family or followers of Caefea', where the Saxon *wic* is used to mean a specialised farm, usually a dairy farm.

Kersoe

An element of doubt exists as to the true personal name here, although it is certain to be related to Creoda. The second element is from Saxon *hoh* giving 'Cridda's spur of land'.

Kidderminster

Seven significant listings of this name are found from Domesday in 1086 up to the Pipe Rolls of 1227 – *Chideminstre, Kedeleministre, Kideministra, Kedemenistra, Kydeministr, Kidelministr* and *Kideministre*. Such a number may contribute to the uncertainty regarding the true personal name here, for this could be either 'Cydda's minister' or 'Cydela's minister', a reference to the monastery which was once found here. The name of Kidderminster gained renown from the eighteenth century with the birth of its famous carpet-making industry and the development of such family firms such as Brinton, Grosvenor and Tomkinson. Just how rapidly this industry grew becomes apparent when one considers that the first factory to produce carpets was built in 1735, yet by 1772 there were over seventeen hundred working looms here. This was a natural follow-on to the cloth-weaving that had existed locally since at least the thirteenth century, including the production of many items from Spanish poplins and arras to frieze and prunellas.

The name of **Aggborough**, also the name of the stadium of one of the newest members of the Football League, Kidderminster Harriers, is seen as *Akberewe* in 1275 and *Agberrow* in 1340. Identical to the origins of Aggberrow Wood (*see* Bushley) this is Saxon *ac-beorg* '(place at or by) the hill where oak trees grow'.

The Severn Valley Railway at Kidderminster.

Also near Kidderminster, from Old English *cald-wyll*, 'the cold spring', comes the modern name of **Caldwell**. There is, as in many towns throughout the land, a **Chester Street**. As with other place-names this element was used to denote the Roman influence. Hence we would presume this to be a Roman road; however, in this case there is no archaeological or documented evidence to suggest the Romans ever attempted to enhance the surface of this trackway.

Today only seen in the name of **Eymore Wood**, this place-name is 'the island moor'. Now the three elements of 'island, moor and wood' would seem an odd combination for one cannot have a moor and a wood at the same place, and as the island in question is in the Severn it cannot be large enough to support anything which could be regarded as a moor or a wood. However this is the origin of the name, and thanks to ancient documents an explanation is possible. The place-name originally applied to a region containing an area of moorland and a wood, and one boundary of this region was a part of the River Severn with a reasonably sized island.

Hurcot is a typical, if uncommon, Saxon name derived from 'the shepherd's cottage(s)'. **Hoarstone Farm** clearly stands on the site of a former 'boundary stone', from which it is derived. Since the times of pagan worship it has been deemed prudent to appease whichever deity is believed to hold the key to a successful growing season. There would have been an actual stone (or stones) at one time. It would have marked the point (or one of them) at which religious leaders would perform the required rites, rather than being a boundary marker in the modern sense. **Puxton** is derived from the Saxon for 'goblin's farmstead' – not a goblin of folklore but a personal name, either derived from or used as a nickname.

The Barrel may have been one of the earliest pub signs to feature a man-made item, instead of the earlier barley, hops, etc. **The Blue Bell** is actually associated with a church, the Bell element being obvious, while blue has always been the colour associated with the Church. Although the spring flower is often depicted on the sign, there is no reason to believe any Blue Bell public house was derived from the woodland bloom.

The **Bulls Head** is widespread, with several additions. The name is truly one of the earliest and, despite the later associations, has its origins in the papal bull (Latin *bulla*), the leaden seal attached to the pope's edicts. The **Cavalier Tavern** may well have taken its name from the Royalists of the seventeenth century who fought for Charles I (not necessarily the battle fought near this place, but maybe an inn which once stood on this site or nearby). The term 'cavalier' was originally used reproachfully, although it is used in a rather different sense today. The Coopers Company dates from the sixteenth century, although the ancient craft of making barrels, casks and tubs is almost as old as civilisation itself. The link with brewing is clear, with the crest of the tradesmen being shown outside the **Coopers Arms**.

A popular ballad gave rise to the name of **The Old House At Home**, relaying the feeling of peace and safety to those serving their country, particularly those away from these shores.

Kings Areley

Despite the different spelling from that of Upper and Lower Arley, the origins are the same in Old English *earn-leah*, 'wood or woodland clearing where eagles are seen'. The additional 'Kings' refers to this place being held by the monarch, added to differentiate from the similarly named Arleys.

Kingsford

This may seem a place-name of obvious origin in 'the river crossing on the king's land'. However, this is not the case. Recorded as *Cenungaford* in 964, this is 'ford at or near the settlement of the family or followers of Cena'. Something of the mistaken belief that the first element related to the king can be seen in the thirteenth-century record of *Keningeford*.

Kington

Domesday's *Chintune* was followed exactly 150 years later by the name appearing in the modern form. The name comes from Old English *cyne-tun*, 'royal manor', a reference to this being among the extensive holdings of the king.

Knighton-on-Teme

The main name comes from Saxon *cnihta-tun*, meaning 'the farmstead of the knights', as evidenced by *Cnihtatun* in 957 and *Cnistetone* in Domesday. It seems this form is erroneous as more than one knight would only be expected if the name referred to a religious order, such as the Knights Templar and there is no evidence of such here. Hence we can safely assume that knight is not plural, but should be in the possessive sense as knight's, meaning this was the farmstead of the knight's servants (for the addition 'Teme' *see* River Teme).

Local place-names include **Bickley**, which is another place-name of Old English origin in '(place at) the woodland clearing of a man called Bica'.

Knightwick

Situated approximately 5 miles west of Bromyard, Knightwick appears as *Cnihtawice* in 964 and *Cnihtewic* in Domesday, showing this to be 'the wic of the knights'. As with Knighton-on-Teme, the 's' is possessive and refers to the servants of the knight. Saxon *wic* refers to a specialised farm, usually a dairy farm.

The footbridge across the Teme at Knightwick.

The cat generously allows the mouse a drink of milk at Cutnall Green, near Knightwick.

Nearby is **Ankardine Hill**, seen in 1275 as *Oncredham* and as *Oncredam* by 1327. Old English *ancra* or *ancer* became Middle English *ancre* or *oncre*, all meaning 'a hermit' or 'anchorite' – either male or female. There is no record of a hermitage here, either in the landscape or in documentation. However, the name of this hill is sure to have originated from 'the hermit's home', or possibly 'the hill of the hermit'.

The public house here known as the **Live & Let Live** was a protest against some (unknown) local incident – probably changes in taxation, or even the opening of a rival pub.

Kyre

Forms such as *Chure*, *Cuer* and *Cura* from the eleventh and twelfth centuries point to this originating from an Old British river-name. This element is found elsewhere in England as Cory and Curry in the modern form. However, the etymology is obscure, although it is safe to assume the meaning is simply a reference to a river, probably descriptive as in fast or white water. The eighteenth-century Kyre Park House has gardens laid out by Capability Brown.

L

Lapal

This is an unusual name, the second element being derived from Saxon *hol* which is normally seen today as the suffix -hall. The earliest forms available adhere more closely to the original Saxon as *Lappol* in 1220, *Laphole* in 1272, and *Lappehol* in 1276. Thus the meaning here is '(place at) Hlappa's hollow', referring to a low-lying region.

Laughern Brook

As with many river-names this is of Old British or Celtic origin, recorded as *Lawern* in 757 and *Lawerna* in 1253. Clearly derived from the word for 'fox' and related to Welsh *llywarn*, and *louuern* which is found in both Old Breton (an early language of the people of Brittany) and Old Cornish, the reference is somewhat obscure. Perhaps the intention was to refer to the river being 'sly' or 'cunning', both traits traditionally associated with foxes, suggesting that Laughern Brook was an unreliable source of water. While the definition is certain, we can only assume the inference was to the possibility of this potential water supply failing in dryer months, as there is insufficient volume to cause any major concern of flooding.

The brook gives its name to the village of **Laughern** and to **Temple Laughern**, the latter once held by the Master of the Temple.

Leadon, River

As with Laughern Brook this is also a British river-name. Listed as *Ledene* in 972 and *Leden* in 1248, this is derived from Old British *litano* meaning 'broad' and is related to the Welsh *llydan* with the same meaning.

Leigh

A common name derived from Old English *leah*, although it is more often found as a second element. Such is the case here, for in 972 this place is listed as *Beornothesleah*, but losing the personal name by the time of the Domesday survey. Hence this 'woodland clearing' was formerly associated with a man called Beornnoth.

Old-fashioned stone road sign at Leigh.

Leigh Sinton is situated at the southern end of Leigh parish. Here the addition is nothing to do with the family who were in residence but, as shown from the record as *Sothyntone Lega*, is 'the place south of the hill'. **Braces Leigh** features the name of a well-known Worcestershire family (correctly known as the de Braiose) who held land here. The estate passed to the Lygon family by marriage in 1419.

The Pale recalls an estate here, the large house of that name having been built by a man who made his fortune as a baker. A pale was the long wooden shovel on which the dough was placed into the oven and later used to remove the baked loaves.

Lindridge

Dating from the eleventh century, we find the record of *Lynderycge* which is from the Saxon *lind-hrycg*. Thus this is 'the lime trees growing on, or near, a ridge of land'.

Welsh *onen* refers to an 'ash tree', and is the origin of **Oney Coppice**. Other places and rivers in Shropshire and Herefordshire (together with this place) once stood on the ancient border with Wales. **Penhull** is another hill-name which is derived from the Celtic *penn*, 'hill', and Old English *hyll*, the Saxon addition as they were unaware of the meaning of the Celtic name. **Dumbleton** near here is of Saxon derivation, being 'Domwulf's farmstead'.

Littleton, North, Middle and South

If in reading this book you have learned that the most common Saxon suffix found in English place-names (that of -*tun*) means 'farmstead', then you can easily guess the origin of the name of Littleton. Up to and including Domesday we find *Litletona, Lytletun, alia Litletun* and *Liteltun*. By the mid-thirteenth century there is evidence of three settlements in *Middleton, Northlittleton* and *Sutlitinton*. There is no reason to think the three were in any way connected, other than by the name. It seems illogical to assume that three separate 'small farmsteads' would have been founded by the same family or group, for this would have been a highly inefficient way to divide the labour. Hence they were most likely completely independent sites sharing a reasonably common place-name.

Longdon

This place is named after a natural feature near Tredington and is a common place-name element describing the 'long hill', and thus also given as the name of the settlement which grew up here. Longdon Hill near Bengeworth has identical origins, but in this case has acquired the explanatory 'Hill'.

The River Severn's tidal influence extended as far inland as Longdon in the days before modern flood controls. Marshland near here, once covered during a tidal flood, still has plants growing there which would be expected to be seen in coastal regions.

Lulsley

Lolleseie and *Lulleseia* show this to be '(place at) Lull's island or land in a marsh'. The personal name is followed by the Saxon *eg*, ostensibly 'island' but also used in the sense of any dry ground within a predominantly marshy region.

Lye

Recorded as Lega in 1275, this name is identical with that of Leigh, from Saxon *leah* '(place at) the woodland clearing'.

M

Madresfield

With Domesday's *Madresfeld* and *Metheresfeld* a century later the only early forms of note, the first element remains uncertain. It may well be the personal name Maethhere or Saxon *maethere* – the latter giving us 'the mower's field', i.e. where grass was cut for fodder.

The second element of Madresfield, Saxon *feld*, is always found as field in modern names. The Saxon feld differed from the modern field in that the area was not necessarily enclosed, as is always the case today, and the feld was invariably used for growing a mix of crops and not for livestock or a single crop as seen today.

The region known as **Frisland** is a name which has similar examples in the north of England in place-names influenced by Scandinavian settlers in the region which became known as Danelaw. However, this is certainly of Saxon origin and is 'land where furze or gorse grows abundantly'.

Malvern, Great, Little and Link

The two places retain their separate identities despite there being no discernible boundary between the two today, save for the road signs. The settlements are referred to as *Maelfern* in 1030, *Malferna* in 1086, *Maluernia* in 1130, and *Magna Malvernain* in 1228 with *Parva Malverna* in 1232. *Magna* and *Parva* are Latin for 'great' and 'small' respectively, while Malvern Link takes its distinguishing characteristic from Saxon *hlinc* '(place at) the ledge, terrace'.

These places take their name from the prominent hills; there are signs of habitation since man first abandoned the way of life of the hunter-gatherer in Britain. Indeed the Malvern Hills would have been a much-envied site for a hill-fort, for they are incapable of allowing the growth of trees, other than on the lower slopes. Hence the inhabitants would have had the luxury of being able to see the approach of any potential threat from other tribes, and could follow the progress of potential prey animals making their way through the vast woodlands which stretched almost unbroken to every horizon.

That the upper reaches of the Malvern Hills were always devoid of all but the most diminutive vegetation is known not only from archaeological evidence, but also from the name of Malvern. As with so many landmarks such as hills and rivers,

Road sign at Malvern.

the name is derived from Old British meaning 'bare hill'. This tongue was closely related to the Cornish, Breton (the native language of those inhabiting the region now known as Brittany in France), and to modern Welsh as seen by *moel-fryn* which means 'bare hill'. In earlier times *moel* was *mel* in Old Welsh, the first syllable of Malvern representing some (uncertain) intermediate form between *mailo* and *moel.*

There is one further record of these settlements dating from 769. This appears as *Themse* which is clearly unrelated to any form of Malvern. It is safe to assume that the reference is to a temporary or short-lived settlement which took its name from one of the streams which cascade down the slopes. It is so close to other river-names such as Teme, Tame, Tyne, and Thames (the origins of which are discussed under the River Teme), that we can be fairly certain this is the case, even if the location of the lost settlement is unknown.

Malvern Link was a settlement known for its pottery in the time of the Romans. During the Saxon era it became predominantly a farming community, something which had changed little by the reign of Elizabeth I. In the seventeenth century **Link Walk** was home to a glover who farmed his own land and was official keeper of the local chase; the skins of the deer were used and the leather clearly worked in **Tanhouse Lane.**

Alicante Close, Harbinger Avenue, Shirley Close and **Challenger Close** are all named from varieties of tomato, for years a staple crop in Worcestershire. **Foley**

Terrace is named after the family who had a large estate here during the nineteenth century. Lady Emily Foley, the fourth daughter of the Duke of Montrose, the lady of the manor is remembered by **Graham Road**, her maiden name. The Earl and Countess of Zetland also left their mark on the maps of Malvern in **Zetland Road**, still the final road or street-name in an alphabetical listing.

Langland Avenue is named after William Langland, whose most famous work *The Vision of Piers the Ploughman* had its first of three versions published in 1362. He was educated at the Priory of Great Malvern.

Lechmere Crescent recalls one of Malvern's most famous sons, Sir Edmund Anthony Harley Lechmere. An impressive list of credentials includes a position as senior partner of Worcester Old Bank, before joining the conflict in the Balkan Wars. He was made Commander of the Servian Order of the Takova, Knight of the Holy Sepulchre, Knight Commander of the Order of St John of Jerusalem, and Knight of Malta, later becoming MP for West Worcestershire (1876–92) and for South Worcestershire (1892–4). The site of the Church of St Gabriel at Hanley Green was donated by him, and it was Sir Edmund's money which paid for the beautiful chapel adjoining Rhydd Court.

Another famous Malvern resident was the composer Edward Elgar. From 1891 to 1899 he lived with his wife Caroline Alice and his only daughter Carice at Forti, in Alexandra Road, where he wrote the *Enigma Variations* which earned him

The Enigma Fountain – commemorating Elgar, his famous Enigma Variations and Malvern as a spa.

global acclaim. From here he moved to **Wells Lane** and the house he had built, Craeglea. The name may sound Saxon, but means nothing as it was simply an anagram of their family name together with their initials. Later the house name was transferred to a housing development near **Pickersleigh Road**, although of no geographical significance. Would Elgar have considered the use of his house name a greater tribute than his portrait on the reverse of the £20 note?

The Rhydd is a place-name which seems to be of Welsh derivation; however, this would have come from *rhyd* meaning 'ford' which is unfounded as the river here was at least 6 ft (and up to twice that depth), the closest ford being at Clevelode further north. There is an Old English *ridde* meaning 'cleared land', which would fit much better here. Another ancient place-name has today become the footpath known as **The Quabbs**. There is little doubt this is taken from the field which it ran alongside, Quabbs Meadow, itself derived from an Old or Middle English term meaning 'marshy place, or bog'.

Lygon Bank is named from William Lygon, only son of Reginald Pyndar, who took his mother's maiden name of Lygon on becoming heir to Madresfield Court. He represented the county in the Houses of Parliament from 1775 to 1806, and was later created Baron Beauchamp of Powyk in 1806, and Viscount Elmley and Earl Beauchamp in 1815, leading to the naming of **Elmley Close** and **Beauchamp Road**.

The Lansdowne Crescent and Link End areas of the town were landholdings of John Bellars in the middle of the eighteenth century. His family later worked Fold Farm in Portland Road. **Bellar's Lane** was named in his memory, although the modern form has the name incorrectly spelled with the possessive 's'.

In November 1939 the RAF station at Pale Manor was founded, together with associated buildings in St Andrews Road which was occupied in May 1941 by the training base of HMS Duke. This episode in Malvern history is commemorated by **Duke Street**.

Tibberton Road was named in honour of W. P. Price of Tibberton, chairman of the Great Malvern Hotel Company, who developed the roads from roads from the railway hotel and the station. (The hotel and the station were connected by a corrugated iron-covered passage; partially submerged, it certainly earned its nickname of 'the worm'.) At almost the same time in 1867 the Conservative Land Society, chairman Viscount L.C. Ranelagh, developed the estate around **Ranelagh**, **Merick** and **Goodson Roads**. The station hotel owed much to the efforts of Dr Gully, who also headed the driving force behind the Imperial Hotel, which became Malvern Girls' College in 1919, and is remembered by **Imperial Road**.

Broad's Bank remembers the efforts of Thomas Broad and his son Charles. From the 1880s the family were at the forefront of building work in Malvern for over thirty years. Charles also launched a scheme for a funicular railway from **Foley Terrace** to the **Worcestershire Beacon**. Whether owing to lack of funds or the outbreak of the First World War is not clear, but the project (although virtually signed and sealed) never got off the ground.

Wykewane recalls one William de Wykewan, who died in the thirteenth century. A fragmented tombstone was found in 1863 underneath the blocked-up doorway of the church. There is a documented record of a gentleman of this name who was ordered to the Priory of Aucote after being released from the prison-house of the Abbot of Westminster. Doubtless he visited Malvern on many occasions, and could well have died and been buried here. However the missing piece(s) of the tombstone make(s) certain identification of the man impossible, and it is safe to assume the name probably owes as much to a fanciful legend than to available facts.

Barnard's Green House was certainly standing by 1677, and was situated near the spot where the roads from Malvern, Poolbrook and Guarlford converged near **Hastings Pool**. The pool is so-named from Sir Charles Hastings, founder of the British Medical Association, who spent his retirement here until his death in 1866. **Hastings Road** also commemorates his achievements and his association with the county. **Pounds Bank Road** near here recalls the parish pound, where domestic animals were kept should their owners (or indeed they) break the ancient rules detailing the conditions controlling grazing rights on the common. From what we can discern from the parish records, the pound was most often full or almost full as indiscretions were commonplace. The present place known as

Welcome sign with the famous hills in the background.

Barnard's Green was formerly known as *Merryvale*. The council estates near here were erected on the field of the ancient Moat Court Farm, preserved in the name of **Moat Way**.

Malvern Link was part of the parish of Leigh, where used to live. Earl Somers he was a prominent figure as lord of the manor during the nineteenth century. Road names such as **Somers Park Avenue** and **Somers Road** are a lasting testament to his influence on the area. **Quest Hills Road** is from an ancient name referring to 'hills where gorse abounds'. A small industrial estate grew up around Sandy's spring and the old pathway still known as **Spring Lane**, and the comparatively contemporary **Sandy's Road**.

Clerkenwell Crescent is named from the Clerkenwell estate, a sum of money left by a former reverend who bequeathed the sum so that not less than £20 p.a. be distributed among the poor of the parish. Should the sum not be paid, then the property would also revert to the charity, which it duly did soon enough. The trust was receiving almost £300 annually by the mid-nineteenth century and reached ever greater heights in later years.

Hornyold Avenue and **Hornyold Road** are named after the **Hornyold Arms Hotel**, itself taking its name from the family who were lords of Hanley Castle. As Roman Catholics, the Hornyolds were at a distinct disadvantage in Elizabethan times, but still managed to accumulate huge areas of land. The hotel was formerly known as the Admiral Benbow, the building enjoying a new lease of life when turned into flats during the 1960s.

The town's link to the Royal Engineers is noted in several road names, including those of **Bawdsey Avenue**, **Matravers Road**, **Steamer Point**, and **Orford Way**. **Hospital Road** needs no explanation: suffice to say the town's first hospital was opened in 1868, was entirely reliant on gifts of money, linen, etc., to survive, and operated as best it could without modern surgical techniques and antibiotics to accommodate a maximum of six male and six female patients at any one time.

Although she lived in Malvern for only ten years, the influence on Malvern by the Right Honourable Lucy Joan Cavendish Scott, Lady Howard de Walden, was considerable. Her efforts saw much building work still in evidence today, and the creation of employment for local people and those from neighbouring villages. Daughter of the fourth Duke of Portland, she inherited a vast fortune from her father after her siblings died without issue. The land held by the family included the prime London sites of Harley Street, Cavendish Square and Portland Square, with **Portland Road** being named in memory of her considerable achievements.

Harcourt Road remembers Mary, Countess Harcourt, who is known to have marked out more hill paths than any other individual. She also built at least two shelters on the hills, one on the southern slopes of Worcestershire Beacon and a second atop Pinnacle Hill, and was only prevented from adding to her achievements by the vociferous objections of those who owned the land. The aforementioned shed on Pinnacle Hill was the scene of a tragedy in 1826. The iron roof attracted a lightning strike, killing four members of the Woodyatt and Hill families from Hereford and Dymock.

Werstan Close is named after the saint to whom the church known as the Priory is dedicated. Over nine hundred years old, the Norman pillars dominate the view as one enters through the main door, although four stained-glass windows show the building of the earlier church by St Werstan. Traditionally said to have been martyred by Danish (or Welsh) invaders, his chapel is believed to have been near St Ann's Well at the top of the ninety-nine steps. Archaeological evidence does show a chapel once stood here. In the sixteenth century Leland expressed his doubts as to the accuracy of Werstan's involvement in the founding of the priory. Today it is accepted that his involvement is limited to an embellishment of the facts to explain the allocation of lands for religious purposes.

Hangman's Hill is reached along **Hangman's Lane**: predictably there were once gallows located here. These were erected on the orders of the forest court, who met at Hanley Castle to sit in judgement on all offences pertaining to the forest. Much of the supposed severity of the sentences of the day is overstated; indeed the gallows themselves were probably erected as a threat or warning to prevent misdemeanours, rather than in constant use, for major offences must have been rare.

The Malverns stand on the border with neighbouring Herefordshire. Here maps show the existence of **Red Earls Dyke**, a reference to Gilbert de Clare, Earl of Gloucester and known as the Red Knight. In about 1290 he married Joan d'Acres, daughter of Edward I, who gave the Forest of Malvern to de Clare. The Bishop of Hereford held neighbouring lands and disagreements over boundaries soon arose, the bishop seemingly content to say nothing when the king held the forest. Eventually agreement was reached and the boundary was marked by the cutting of a ditch. Similarly the appropriately named **Shire Ditch** marked the boundary with neighbouring Gloucestershire.

The **Gloster Arms** at Malvern Link is not a spelling error. The crest shown is that of the Gloucestershire Regiment, who for some reason prefer the spelling of 'Glosters'. An early landlord or benefactor would have been a former member of the regiment. **The Green Dragon** is not a reference to the story of St George but commemorates the earls of Pembroke who feature this mythical beast on the family crest. Often humorously depicted on pub signs of today, the original **Nag's Head** would have indicated this small pony was available for hire here.

The Portobello, once a common sign, commemorates the achievements of Admiral Edward Vernon (1684–1757). He became a national hero in 1739 when he captured Porto Bello in Panama from the Spanish, despite only having six ships under his command. Vernon was elected a member of parliament several times, first as the representative for Penryn in Cornwall and later for Ipswich. Any link with Malvern is at best tenuous, and the pub was probably named in honour of the engagement (maybe a favourite narrative of an early innkeeper).

Many pubs have the element 'horseshoe', sometimes in the plural. At Malvern is the **Three Horseshoes**, an echo from the days when the village blacksmith was often found next to the inn and advertising a re-shoeing service available to travellers – hence three and not four horseshoes.

Finally in our look at Malvern and its place-names we come to Lady Lyttleton. Born Apphia Witts in 1743, the second daughter of Broome Witts, she was engaged at the age of twenty-four to her cousin Richard Witts, who spent much of his time away with the East India Company. In 1769 she sailed to India for the marriage, only to find he had died during her voyage. Grief-stricken and penniless she met Colonel James Peach, an army veteran and governor of Calcutta. A whirlwind romance saw them married the following January, only for him to die ten days after contracting a fever six months later. She returned to England and went to live at Shenstone, where she met the Honourable Thomas Lyttleton – a notorious rake of the day who was obviously only interested in the wealth she had inherited from Colonel Peach. He managed to convince her he was a reformed character and they married in 1772. After the wedding his delight at getting his hands on her money clearly got to him, for he made his way to the wedding carriage without her and his apology for his oversight saw Lyttleton address his new bride as 'Mrs Peach'. Within months she was alone again and living with her

The Malvern hills dominate this part of the country. (George Hobbs)

father-in-law, George Lyttleton, at Hagley Hall. She came to Malvern around the turn of the century, eventually settling in the home she had built, which she named **Peachfield Lodge** in memory of her beloved first husband.

Lady Lyttleton was a leading personality as Malvern grew from village to town. Rarely leaving her home, where her role as hostess was legendary, she did venture out when in her eighties to Madresfield Court, and charmed the Duchess of Kent and a young Princess Victoria to such a degree they wrote and thanked her personally for their 'unforgettable summer'. Despite a number of heart-breaking setbacks in her early life, Lady Lyttleton lived to see her ninety-sixth year. Reports seem to indicate most of the town turned out to her funeral, shops were closed, the crowds spilled out into the churchyard and many others watched the funeral procession from windows, doorways and even rooftops to witness the end of an era in Malvern's history.

Mamble

Here is another settlement taking its name from a geographical feature, in this instance a hill. Listings of *Momela gemaera* in *c.* 957, and Domesday's *Mamele*, point to Momela as being the genitive of a folk-name, itself derived from an earlier Old British name. While the exact reference of the early name is unknown, we can be certain it will be related to the word *mam*, literally meaning 'hill' but always used to refer to a 'breast-shaped hill' – although this can often be misleading as such a shape may only be visible from certain angles (particularly the side the settlement is sited). This element is common to a number of hill-names, and is still on the maps of Derbyshire today in its original form in the shape of **Mam Tor**.

Clows Top, **Clows Cottage** and **High Clows** all have their origins from a family name. Records from the early part of the fourteenth century speak of the Clowe family (also written as Clouse) having an estate here. **Spilsbury Hill** has a name which refers to the settlement which grew up alongside here rather than to the hill itself, for this is 'Spil's fortified place'.

Martin Hussingtree

At first glance it appears that Martin is the manorial addition; however, this is not the case here. There are two relevant listings, both dating from 972 as *Meretun* and *Husantreo*. These are of Saxon origin meaning 'farmstead by a lake' and 'the tree of Husa' respectively. It may be that these were once two separate places which expanded and were eventually indistinguishable, but it seems more likely that Husa's tree was a landmark (possibly a boundary marker) so well known it became part of the name.

Martley

Mertlega, Maertleages ecge, Mertelai, Mardelege and *Martheleg* are among the forms found from the eleventh to the thirteenth centuries. Coming from Old English *mearth-leah*, this is '(place at) the woodland clearing frequented by martens'. Although still found in the more remote parts of Britain, and as a protected species numbers are on the increase, the chances of seeing a pine marten in the vicinity of Martley today are remote. Indeed the place-name seems a little odd in that the pine marten is a solitary creature and, although borders can overlap, there is something strange about several martens being noticed within the same clearing, especially to a degree where the place was renowned and thus named for it.

An interesting name near Martley is **The Noake**, which comes from the Saxon for '(place) at the oak'. Clearly this must have been of significance, despite being a reasonably small area. Although not documented as such, it is safe to assume the oak in question was either a boundary marker and/or a place of worship – both for Christians and earlier religions.

Three similar place-names have their origins in 'Pudda's ford'. While the ford disappeared from maps long ago, the Saxon gentleman is still remembered by **Pudford Hill**, **Pudford Farm** and **Pudford Coppice**.

An interesting road name at Martley, of unknown origins.

Mathon

There is no doubt that this is derived from Saxon *matme,* which means 'treasure, or gift'. Early records include *Maima* in Domesday and as *Maithine* in 1275. However, in just what context such a name refers to Mathon is a mystery. Some have suggested the region was given as a gift – perhaps a dowry – but unless more clues surface, we shall never be any wiser.

A manor referred originally to a unit of land, which could contain one or more parishes, and was run by a manorial lord from the manor house, court or hall. It seems Domesday's entry of a virgate (approximately 30 acres) of waste land was held by Walter Ponther. Any land termed 'waste' by Domesday simply meant it was either not used as agricultural land, or was unfit for growing crops (the latter seems the case here). This would appear to be the first reference to what was to become **Farley**. Derived from the Old English *fern-leah,* this is 'the woodland clearing where ferns abound'.

Mitton, Upper and Lower

Listed as *Mettune* in Domesday, *Mutton* in 1227, and *Ouermitton* in 1221, the name of Mitton comes from the Old English for 'farmstead at the junction of the streams'. It seems likely that Lower Mitton was the original settlement, Upper Mitton being a satellite settlement most likely to be an agricultural establishment used principally for storing crops or sheltering livestock.

Moseley

Domesday's *Museleie* is for once a better example than that of *Moseleia* in 1195. This place-name originates in Old English or Saxon *mus-leah,* '(place at or near) the woodland glade infested by mice'. Rodent populations are governed almost exclusively by the source of food, and so we can assume that the mice population exploded after the human farmers managed to inadvertently provide them with a vast supply of food.

Mucklow Hill

Often heard named as Mucklow's Hill, the name seems to be regaining the possessive 's' of the Saxon era. While the most likely origin is '(place at) Muca's low', there is also a chance that a family name has had influence, for John Moghlowe is recorded as holding land here in 1424.

N

Naunton Beauchamp

From Old English *niwe-tun*, this is 'the new farmstead'. We find this recorded as *Niuuantune* in 972, *Newentune* in Domesday, and *Newenton Beauchamp* in 1370. Presumably there was an earlier farmstead, yet this is now either lost, was abandoned at the time for the new site, or relates to a surviving (unknown) village.

As expected, the addition refers to the manorial holding here by William de Bellocampo in 1167.

Newbold-on-Stour

Of similar origins to Naunton, this is seen as *Nioweboldan* in 991 and *Newbold-on-Stoure* in 1383. Here the name tells us of 'the new building'; again there was presumably an earlier version (possibly on the same site), but this has never been proven.

(For the river-name, *see* Stour.)

Newland

The origins are not quite as obvious as one would think. *La Newelande* in 1221, and *Newelond* in 1327 show this particular '(place in) new land' was probably used to indicate 'newly cleared or newly acquired land'.

Locally are found **Limberrow Cottages**, which take their name from the Saxon for this locality which they knew as '(place at) the hill where lime trees grow'.

Northfield

Now considered a part of the West Midlands and a suburb of Birmingham, Northfield was a part of Worcestershire for centuries. It is a simple enough name to define for it means exactly what it says, except the second element is Saxon *feld,* which had more or less the same uses as the modern field but would rarely be enclosed.

As this place was labelled 'northern', we can assume the place was associated with a nearby settlement. However, it is difficult to suggest which that may have been as there was probably a 'southern feld' somewhere which led to the name, while there is no way of knowing the direction of Northfield in relation to the larger original settlement.

Northwick

As with Northfield, it is unclear exactly what this place was north of and thus difficult to determine with which other settlement it was associated. However, the name is clearly 'the northern wic', where Saxon *wic* refers to a specialised farm, much of the time devoted to dairy produce. The earliest record is as *Norowica* in 964.

Norton

Another 'north' name, this time one of the most common place-names in England, this is 'the northern farmstead' from Old English *nord-tun*. There is a twelfth-century marble lectern in the church which was found near the site of Evesham Abbey and transported to Norton.

Several examples are found within Worcestershire's boundaries. Norton near Evesham is found as early as 709 in the form of *Nortona*. **Norton Juxta Kemsey** is *Nordtun* in 989 and *Norton juxta Kemeseye* in 1346, with *juxta* the Latin for 'nearby, next to'. (The origins of Kempsey are discussed under its own entry.) **Kings Norton** is now part of the West Midlands. The original 'northern farmstead' of Domesday was among the lands belonging to the king and is first noted as such in the place-name in 1221.

O

Oddingley

Three elements have combined to produce the modern name, 'personal name'-*inga-leah* all of which are Saxon. The modern form is closer to the ninth-century listing of *Oddingalea* than those of *Odduncalea* in 963 and Domesday's *Oddunclei*. Here was to be found '(place at) the woodland clearing of the family or followers of a man called Odda'.

Offenham

Offeham, *Uffaham* and *Offenham* from 709, 714 and 1086 respectively show this to be 'the homestead of a man called Offa or Uffa'.

Locally we find **Faulk Mill**, which is not a personal name but is derived from the same origin as the modern 'folk', here meaning 'mill of the people'. This is quite unusual, for the watermill of the day was a highly profitable asset, inevitably under the ultimate control of the lord of the manor. Here it appears the mill was given for the community as a whole.

Oldbury

The only early form available is as *Oldebure* in 1270. This is certainly 'the old fort' and would refer to a pre-Roman hill-fort, so it is somewhat surprising that other forms are not found pre-dating that of the late thirteenth century.

Ombersley

Listings of 706, 714 and 817 as *Ambreslege*, *Ambresleie* and *Ombersetene gemaere* respectively are useful, but still mean the first element here is somewhat uncertain. It could refer to a Saxon personal name and mean this is '(place at) the woodland clearing associated with the family or followers of a man called Odda'. However, it is possible that this element is Old English *amer*, in which case this would make it '(place at) the woodland clearing where bunting abound'.

Barnhall is a name of interest to those studying the origins of place-names. The name means, predictably, 'the place of a barn'. However the early record of 816 as

Bernes ende is one of the earliest known where 'end' is used in a place-name, always used in the sense 'locality'. While derived from '(place at) the woodland glade of the wild boar', **Borsley Farm** still retains much of its original meaning today.

Two Saxon place-names are easy to define. **Suddington** is a reference to an overspill settlement as 'the southern farmstead'. **The Lyth** is an unusual element to find standing alone: normally found in combination with a personal name, this is '(the place at or by) a slope or hill side'.

Bournes Dingle has a common second element used then as it is today. The first element is a manorial affix, referring to Sir John Bourne who held this manor in the sixteenth century. Another place-name of similar origins is **Gardner's Grove**, which belonged to the Gardener family by 1604.

The two similar place-names of **Sytchampton** and **Tytchney** may seem to have a common first element. Nothing could be further from the truth, though, for the former is derived from Saxon for 'the farmstead by the watercourse', yet the latter is 'settlement at the place where two roads meet'. There can be no doubt the name of **Chatley** is of Old English derivation meaning 'Ceatta's woodland clearing'.

The Bible relates the words spoken by Christ to St Peter: 'I will give unto thee the keys of the kingdom of heaven.' Christian heraldry commonly depicts the crossed keys, including the papal coat of arms, and with the close historical relationship between the church and public houses it is no surprise to find the **Cross Keys** public house here (and elsewhere).

Ombersley: a common pub name, bearing a famous local name.

St Andrew's Church, Ombersley.

There is not one single record of a wild reindeer anywhere near Ombersley, so why a pub in the village should be called the **Reindeer Inn** is unknown. The only possible explanation is that the splendid antlers of this animal may have been used as a sign, or as ornamentation over the fireplace within. Yet again the name may merely have been brought by a new landlord.

Orleton

Domesday's *Alretune* and *Ealretun* from a transcript of an early eleventh-century document point to the name being derived from the Saxon *alor-tun*, 'the farmstead where alder trees grow'.

Overbury

As *Uferebreodun* in 875 and *Overberie* in 1086 this place is 'the upper fortification'. While there is no indication as to what this place was 'upper' of, or if there was ever a 'lower' fortification, we do know this refers to an early British settlement, or rather to the earthwork constructed by them as defence.

P

Pedmore

This was the earthwork to a very early camp on Wychbury Hill. However, the name doesn't reflect this part of Stourbridge at all. From Domesday we find *Pevermore*, by 1176 it had become *Pubemora*, and at the end of the thirteenth century *Pebbemore*. This is undoubtedly 'Pybba's moor'. There is evidence of a prehistoric camp on Wychbury Hill in the form of earthworks.

Nearby **Henmarsh Wood** is the only remnant of a name which was coined to describe 'the marsh frequented by wildfowl'.

Pendock

Although the earliest records are as *Peonedoc* in 875 and *Penedoc* in 967, the name pre-dates the Saxon era considerably. This is an Old British or Celtic name related to Welsh and consisting of *penn-heidiogg*, meaning 'of barley' or 'barley field'. Hence this would have been '(place at) the hill where barley was grown' (or possibly it implies '(place at) the end of the barley field'). Either would suit as it stands on the lower slope of Malvern Hill.

Pensax

It is clear that this name was coined by Celtic neighbours and not by those who lived here. The first element is the same as that found in Pendock, the name being a combination of *penn-Sachson* '(place at) the hill of the Saxons', and is recorded as *Pensaxan* and *Pensex* in 1231.

Penn Hall is found here, noted as *Penhyll* and *Penhull* in 1221. Again we find the Celtic or Welsh *penn*, but here the second element is Old English *hyll*, both of which mean 'hill'.

Pensham

The two relevant early forms are *Pedneshamme* in 972 and *Pendesham* in Domesday. 'Peden's homestead' features a personal name which is derived from Peada, and may well have been used as a nickname.

Peopleton

The first element is probably a personal name, 'farmstead associated with the family or followers of a man called Pyppel', from records as *Piplincgtun* in 972, *Piplintune* in 1086, and *Puplinton* in 1254. However, if the first element is actually Old English *pyppel,* then the meaning is very different as 'farmstead near the stream with pebbles'.

Pepper Woods

Recorded as *Pyperode* in ancient documents, the first element here is derived from Saxon *fyhthe* which is used to describe 'sparse woodland and scrub', here with the addition of *wudu* 'wood'.

Perdiswell

Although there may be some differences of opinion regarding the personal name in evidence here, the twelfth-century listing of *Perdeswell* probably suggests this was '(place at) Preed's spring'.

Near here, at **Barrow Cop**, have been found prehistoric ornaments, although no trace of the barrow remains. A barrow, or tumulus, was a man-made mound of earth covering a burial chamber (or chambers), normally built on or alongside a ley line. These early people believed the trackways known as ley lines were sources of an energy emanating from the earth itself. In order to maximise the benefits of this energy, burial chambers were always built on the ley lines. Today those who still feel there is some earth-force (also used to explain the phenomenon of crop circles) attempt to track these ancient pathways by means of dowsing rods. Here the Saxon *copp* means 'head, summit', hence this is 'the hill with a tumulus at the summit'.

Pershore

The earliest forms of Pershore give clues to the origins, even if they fail to answer the primary question of the origins of the place-name. Listed as *Perscoran* in 972, *Prescoran* in 1035, *Persceoran* in 1055, and *Persore* in the 1086 survey known as Domesday, the doubt over the source of the first element remains. The dialect word *persh* is well known to mean 'osier' and is also seen in the later Middle English as *persche*, meaning 'twig'. If this is the correct etymology, then when combined with the Saxon *ora* we find '(settlement at) the bank where osiers grow'. Here the term 'osier' is used to refer to the rod-like twigs of various willows which

Pershore Abbey.

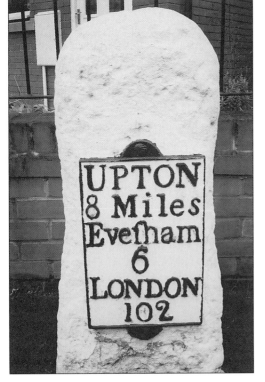

*A new version of an old milestone. The side
road is named after it.*

were used in the making of baskets. Some elements of the parish church originally formed part of the earlier Norman Benedictine monastery.

Nearby stands **Allsborough Hill**, another name of Saxon origin. Here the personal name is not known for certain, but would have been something not unlike '(place at) Aelli's hill'.

The Brandy Cask is not a popular name for a pub. However, the implications are clear, and the resulting sign would have been inexpensive in the early days (*see* the Barrel at Kidderminster). The **Miller's Arms** displays the crest of the trade, almost certainly as an invitation to those associated to enter. Pershore has been famous for its plums for many years, so it is no surprise to find a public house named **The Plum Tree**. Furthermore the fame of the local fruit has spread, for there is a pub called the **Pershore Plum** at Winchester.

Piddle

A place-name recorded as *Pidelet* in Domesday and *Pydele* in 1234 is today named North Piddle. **Wyre Piddle** is seen in only one early historical record, in Domesday as *Pidele*. Both of these places stand on the Piddle Brook, clearly the source of the place-names. Piddle is a river-name of Germanic origin and related to Middle Dutch *pedel*, meaning 'low land, fen land, or marsh'.

The additions in the two place-names are fairly self-explanatory – one clearly the northern settlement, the second in some way associated with Wyre Forest (*see* Wyre) which may have extended as far as to here or perhaps this refers to the settlement closer to the forest.

Traces of the moat around the manor house can still be seen at North Piddle.

Pinvin

Although only one record of any relevance to defining the name remains, that of 1187 as *Pendefen* is doubtless '(the place at or by) Penda's fen'.

Of course the **Coach and Horses** public house refers to the 'high-speed' transport system of the seventeenth century. It does not necessarily refer to a stopping point but is just as likely to have been adopted by a man who became an innkeeper after being employed on the coaches in some capacity.

Pirton

This name is found in several places around the south and west of England, this particular place being recorded as *Pyritune* in 972 and *Peritune* in Domesday. Clearly derived from Old English *pirige-tun*, this is either used to mean 'the farmstead where pear trees grow' or possibly, simply 'pear orchard'.

Powick

This village on the Teme south of Worcester has early forms such as *Poincguuic* in 972 and *Poiwic* in 1086. This is 'the specialised (or dairy) farm associated with the family or followers of a man called Pohha', from the 'personal name' with Saxon *ing-wic*.

The nearby hamlet of **Bastonford** has sufficient surviving early forms to show this place-name is derived from 'Beorstan's river-crossing'. **Clevelode** has been the site of a trackway since at least Saxon times, as seen by the derivation of the name as 'passage or way, along or by the steep bank'.

The origins of **Cromwells Tavern** depend on when the name was first adopted here (possibly by earlier premises nearby). Clearly a reference to the battles of the English Civil War fought near here, the earliest named may have shown support for the Parliamentarians, or could have been a Royalist statement if coined following the Restoration. What is certain is that the Royalists won the first battle of the English Civil War at Powick Bridge in 1642.

If the **Halfway House** was ever meant literally, it is either inaccurate in describing its position between Malvern and Worcester, or it refers to the midway point between two other places.

Born at Powick in 1708, Dr John Wall headed a team who founded Worcester Porcelain. He experimented until he had perfected a way of imitating the fine china products of the east. Traditionally Dr Wall is seen as the man who pushed Malvern water for its medicinal properties. However, while he certainly had a hand in increasing the popularity of Malvern as a spa town, his influence was minimal.

The electricity works at Powick, built in 1894 and somewhat modernised today. Alongside runs the mill race for the former mill upstream, seen here just before it re-joins the Teme.

Q

Queenhill

There can be no doubt this name means 'royal hill', literally land held by the reigning monarch. However, the modern form shows the wrong gender. Early records are plentiful: *Cynhylle, Cumhille, Cunhille, Queinhill, Kinhill* and *Kunhill* all originate from Old English *cyne-hill*, which certainly refers to a king. However sometimes the place was written as *Quinhill* (or similar), which was misread as 'queen'.

R

Redditch

It is tempting to give the origins as simply 'red-ditch'. Despite one thirteenth-century record of *Rubeo Fossato,* another reference to *la Rededich* shows this to be unlikely. The true origin here is Old English or Saxon *hreod-dic* meaning 'the reed ditch' or 'reedy ditch'.

Redditch is famous for needle-making, which may well have been started by the monks of Bordesley Abbey supplying fish-hooks to boost their finances. The Cistercian abbey was founded here in 1138 and the monks remained until the Dissolution of the Monasteries by Henry VIII.

Headless Cross would suggest that the crossroads on the Ridgeway here was marked by a cross which had either lost or was lacking a top. However, there is a record of a William de Hedley in 1275 and one Simon de Hedleye in 1294 which has led some to believe this originated as 'Headley's Cross'. There are no forms of the name earlier than the thirteenth century, which adds further weight to the

Needle mill and museum at Redditch.

Bordesley Abbey, Redditch. Most of the remains of the church are buried, although the outline is visible from the air.

family name origin theory. Yet crossroad-marking, especially one on such a major and ancient route, would be expected to have existed here since Roman times. It is possible that the 'headless cross' was the result of damage to a replacement marker, or that the 'headless' version was the early marker which was replaced, or even the family name being taken from the place-name.

Further along the Ridgeway is **Crabs Cross**, standing at the junction of the old road from Shrewsbury to London. As with Headless Cross we find a personal name which may be the origin here (or vice versa), one John Crabbe having lived here in 1332. Again early forms are unavailable, but unlike Headless Cross there is no Saxon element which may be an alternative to the personal name. As the crossroads are only 2 miles apart it is easy to see how both would be deemed to have similar origins, which only adds to the confusion. Whatever the true origin of the modern place-names, unlikely to be resolved as there are no earlier forms, logically there would have been markers here from Roman times. Hence it is reasonable to assume that the modern names are different from the earlier place-names, now lost in the mists of time.

The name of **Fox Lydiate** is recorded in about 1300 as *Fox huntley yates*, literally 'the fox-hunter's gate', although 'gate' in this sense would have referred to a simple gap or passage. **Warkwood** is a place-name which means literally 'work wood'. Here the sense is not that carpentry was practised here, but denotes that there was a supply of quality timber to be had.

As a pub name the **Black Horse** has been popular since at least the fourteenth century and has become one of many names which instantly point to a public house. (Someone stating they are off to the 'Black Horse' would never be thought to be going riding, or even to the bank!) Thus this name both audibly and visually doubtless refers to a pub. From the seventeenth century the phrase was also in use as a nickname for the 7th Dragoon Guards, and former members of the regiment who took on the role of inn-keeper in later life would have certainly chosen to name or re-name their hostelry in memory of their earlier life. Similarly the **White Hart** was originally heraldic, although in later times signs often reflected stag-hunting even when the name certainly had nothing to do with such.

The **Eagle** at Crabs Cross is a common name, which is either a Christian or heraldic symbol – either being chosen to represent the lord of the manor, in order to court favour, or to mark his family's patronage. Surprisingly, the **Rising Sun** is another of heraldic origins which invariably points to some link (albeit a tenuous one) with either Edward III or Richard III. A similar name is that of the **Star and Garter**, a reference to the Most Noble Order of the Garter, the highest order of knighthood in the land, established by Edward III in 1348.

Britain's prosperity and subsequent rise to world dominance was based on the wool trade for several centuries. With the vast numbers involved in this industry, from farmers through to the end product, it is no surprise that the **Fleece** remains one of the most widespread of pub names.

> This gate hangs well
> and hinders none.
> Refresh and pay,
> and travel on.

The **Gate Hangs Well** has several examples around the counties of the Midlands. Today seen as a typical, if unusual, name for a public house, the earliest gates would have stood close to a church gate, town gate or even a toll gate.

Redmarley

Together with Redmarley d'Abitot, early forms of these places abound. Between the latter half of the tenth century and the early fourteenth century we find *Ridmerlege, Redmerleie, Rudmerlege, Reodemaereleage, aet Rydemaereleage, Ridmerlege* and *Rudmarleye Dabetot*. The origins here are the Saxon words *hreod-mere* meaning '(place at) the woodland glade near a reedy lake'.

The affix of Redmarley d'Abitot is clearly a reference to the Norman landlord. Here we find Urso d'Abitot held this place in 1086 (*see* Croome d'Abitot.) The region known as **Murrell's End** is named from the Morele family who are known to have been active here during the fifteenth and sixteenth centuries, although no record of the individuals concerned has survived.

A small outlying settlement in Saxon times was known as 'Isenheard's farmstead'. This personal name was originally a nickname, and may have been used as such here, and applied to those of great strength or strong disposition, for it means 'iron hard'. Today this place-name appears as **Inardstone**.

Ribbesford

Early forms, such as *Ribbedford* in 1023 and *Ribeford* in 1086, are surprisingly close to the modern form. From Old English *ribbe-bedd-ford* this is 'ford by a bed or ribwort of hound's tongue'. Neither of these plants had any practical uses, but were easily recognised, especially when in full bloom, hound's tongue having hairy leaves, small reddish-purple flowers, and prickly clinging fruit (taking its name from the shape of its leaves), while ribwort has ribbed leaves, and a dense spike of small whitish flowers.

Ridgeway, The

It has been suggested that this represents a word which reflects the new roads built by the Romans which, unlike existing tracks in Britain, had drainage ditches on both sides and were built to allow the surface water to drain away. Other sources point to these tracks running along a ridge of a hill. This is an ancient track and certainly pre-dates the Romans by several centuries, and the Ridgeway does not run along a ridge of hills for any appreciable distance (certainly no more than any other ancient track). Thus while it is likely that both the hill ridges and the drainage ditches have had a certain influence on the evolution of the name, neither can be considered the true origins which are unknown.

Ripple

From Saxon *ripel*, and recorded as *Rippell* and *Rippel* in the eighth and eleventh centuries respectively, this name has nothing to do with water in the modern sense of the word. Here we find the '(place at) the strip of land'.

Rochford

Although the only record is that of *Recesford* in Domesday, this is certainly from Old English *raecc-ford*, '(place at) the river crossing of the hunting-dog'. Now it seems unlikely that a dog would have any place-named after it, and even more unlikely that this dog would be in the habit of hanging around a ford. Therefore we must assume that this was either a ford regularly used by those who hunted with a pack of such animals, or perhaps this was a nickname given to a man who lived very near here. If the latter is the case it is doubtful that it was meant as a term of affection.

Rock

Sometimes the evolution of a place-name defies any logical progression. This is one such name and has nothing to do with rocks whatsoever. Two records are found, *Ak* in 1224 and the rather different *Roke* thirty-five years later. The two are not as different as it seems at first glance. The clue to the connection is the Old English *aet thaere ace* which means 'at the oak', a reference to the situation near some (unknown) distinctive oak tree.

The region known as **Worsley** tells of the 'pasture for cattle'. This was recorded as *Worfesleahges gemaera*, *Werveslega*, and *Worvesleg* between the tenth and twelfth centuries, which shows the name to be derived from Old English *weorf-leah*, and must have been particularly good pasture producing good-quality dairy produce. The area named **Alton** has undergone considerable contraction since it was founded as 'Aelfwine's farmstead'.

The Bliss Gate refers to the thirteenth-century holdings in the county of the family name de Blez (or Bledis) whose name comes from Blay in Normandy. They left their mark on the landscape with the Gate (Saxon *geat* meaning 'gap or pass') which bears their name.

This region was once the venue of a royal hunt, as evidenced by the public house known as the **Royal Forester Inn**. Further proof of the hunt is found in the name of **Hurtlehill Farm**, which is derived from the Old English for 'clearing where stags are found'. However the name of **Buckridge**, while probably influenced by the hunt, has its origins in flora, not fauna, for this is '(place at) the ridge where beech trees grow'.

Locally we also find **Conningswick Farm**, named from the region settled by the Saxons and known as 'the dairy farm of the family or followers of Cola'. Nearby is **Fernhall's Farm**, where the possessive 's' is a modern corruption as it was mistakenly believed to refer to a former tenant. However from early forms we can see this to be derived from '(place at) the nook of land where ferns abound'. **Hollin Farm** is also easy to mistake for a personal name, whereas the true origin is 'settlement where holly grows'.

Romsley

Even records from 1270 and 1291 as *Romesle* and *Romesleye* respectively hardly make the first element evident, unless you are conversant with the Saxon word *hramsa*, which is related to Middle Low German *ramese* and Norwegian *rams*, referring of course to ramson (*Allium ursinum*), which as any horticulturalist will be aware is wild garlic. Hence Romsley is 'the woodland glade where wild garlic grows'.

The **Sun Inn** is one of the pub names where the simplicity of the sign was a major factor in the choice of the name. More recent 'Sun' names allude to the idea that 'a place in the sun' is the desire of many and is used to suggest a warm welcome is to be found within.

Rous Lench

This was originally just Lench, from a Saxon word meaning 'hill' (*see* Ab Lench). The addition, first seen in 1291 as *Lench Randulph*, is from the Norman French name Randulf and has become corrupted over the intervening centuries.

The name of **Radford** refers to the river crossing on an ancient highway between Alcester and Worcester.

Victorian postbox at Radford bearing the coat-of-arms of a local family.

Rubery

Now a part of the vast conurbation of Birmingham and in the West Midlands, Rubery and the hill with which it shares its name were for centuries an isolated and independent settlement (and a part of Worcestershire). Listed as *Rowberrie* and *Roughberrow* in the sixteenth century, even today the Saxon *ruh-beorg* can be seen to ring true for this place-name means 'the rough hill' – 'rough' being used here in the sense of 'lacking good soil'.

A record of 1452 speaks of *Gynnors Lane*, which is apparently an early form of **Gunners Lane**. This cannot be anything to do with a gun, and a clue to the true origin is found in the 1840 record of *Gin Meadow*. This is a reference to a 'gin', a winching device using a horse walking in a circle to raise coal or peat. In 1275 two brothers lived here, Thomas and Adam le Gynur: here the surname represents 'engineers'. Indeed several local family names suggest that this was the site of an ironworks and/or shallow coal mines. Excavations for constructions in the twentieth century have revealed a layer of peat just a few feet below the surface. **Turves Green**, seen in 1490 as *Turveslond*, shows that peat was cut here for fuel. Below this layer of peat were successive layers of clay and a coal seam, together with unmistakable signs of a bloomerie – the first forge for smelting iron from the ore, leaving less bulk to transport for further smelting to refine the metal. Trade and place-names provide further evidence of the early workings, including the family names of Bloomfield, Blumm and le Colle, together with place-names such as **Colmers Farm** and **Coal Pit Meadow**.

Rushock

If the early forms of *Russococ* and *Rossoc*, from 1086 and 1166 respectively are to be trusted, then this name is derived from the Old English word *ryscuc*. This can be interpreted to refer to '(settlement at or near) a rushy place, or rush bed'.

Rushwick

This place is named from the stream here, which is listed as *Rixuc* in 963. The stream name must mean 'rushy brook', and the place-name is thus 'the special place at the rushy brook'.

S

Salwarpe

Listed as *Salouurpe* in 817 and *Salewarpe* in Domesday, this name probably originates from Old English *salu-wearp* meaning 'dark-coloured silted land'. The name was probably also influenced by the Saxon word *weorpan* meaning 'to throw', literally throwing up silt. Usually the Old English *waesse*, 'alluvial land' is used to describe an area subjected to seasonal floods. This may mean that the Saxon *waesse* was regarded as being beneficial in bringing valuable minerals to replenish the land, while *wearp* referred to an area which was also flooded annually but without adding anything to the agricultural potential.

The **Salwarpe River** probably provided the basis for the place-name, but would have meant something closer to 'sallow, brownish yellow (river)'. Today both are identical, the river-name taking the place-name (in a process known as back-formation), while originally the latter would have been slightly different. A tributary of the Salwarpe is recorded as *Oter burne* in 1038, 'the brook where otters are seen', and is now known as the **Atterburn**. A local name for the Salwarpe River is **Sugar Brook**, a strange name of unknown origin. The suggestion that this arose after a cart carrying sugar along the road from Gloucester broke down, throwing several bags of sugar into the river, was certainly created to fit the name rather than the reverse.

Dyers Bridge crosses the Salwarpe River on the road to Worcester. The name is the only surviving reminder of a former manor of the same name. The earliest record of the family name comes from 1275 where the names of Robert le Deyar and John le Dyere are recorded as residing here. The **Golden Lion Inn** stands on the site of the former manor house. While such a pub name is clearly of heraldic derivation, there is no reason to believe it refers specifically to the Dyer family. **Pulley Farm** here is the only surviving remnant of 'the woodland clearing with a pool'.

Sapey, Lower and Pichard

The name of Sapey is seen as *Sapian* in 781, *Sapie* in Domesday, and *Sapie Pichard* in 1242. The basis here seems to be Old English *sapige* or *saepige* meaning 'sappy' and 'full of sap' respectively. Exactly what this refers to is unknown, but would have been of great relevance so we might assume it to refer to lush pasture.

There are actually three Sapeys, all of which are within a few miles of each other, standing along **Sapey Brook**. Doubtless the name of the brook came about by back-formation from one or all of the settlements. Pichard refers to the family who held this place from at least the thirteenth century, while Lower Sapey is just 3 miles from Upper Sapey, the latter standing across the border in Herefordshire.

The name of **Harpley** is as it may at first seem, for this is 'the harp-shaped woodland clearing'.

Sedgeberrow

Listings as *Segcgesbearuue* in the eighth century and as *Seggesbarue* in Domesday show this to be '(place at) the grove of a man called Secg'. The personal name is suffixed by Old English *bearu*. *Secg* is an Saxon word meaning 'warrior' which was also used as a personal name.

Sedgeberrow was first granted to Worcester church in 777. The present manor house stands on the site of an earlier building which housed the monks.

Selly Oak

Now a suburb of Birmingham, Selly Oak is listed as *Escelie* in Domesday, *Selvele* in 1204, and *Selleg* in 1236. This is a Normanized form of what became the place-name Shelley, both derived from Old English *scylf-leah* meaning '(place at) the woodland glade on a slope or ledge'.

Oak is a comparatively late addition, and has no apparent significance.

Severn, River

The earliest record of this name dates from AD 115 as *Sabrina*. Later found as *Saeferne* in 757, *Habren* in *c.* 800, *Saefern* in 896, *Hefren* in *c.* 1150, *Sauerne* in Domesday, *Saverne* in *c.* 1140, and *Seuerne* in 1205. While the name is known to be identical to the old name of a Bedfordshire stream, and also that of the Sabrann River in Ireland (the old name of the River Lee), the etymology of this extremely ancient river-name is uncertain.

Severn Stoke

Clearly the first element is taken from the river on which the place stands, the origins of which have already been discussed.

Stoke must be the most common word in English place-names. This place is seen as *Stoc* in 972, *Stoche* in Domesday, and *Savernestok* in a record dated 1212. The exact meaning of Old English *stoc* is nothing more complex than 'place'. This

The River Severn at Holt Fleet.

should be taken to infer a place of some significance, although just what was special about this (or any) Stoke is lost on us today.

Other stokes have had meanings suggested, such as 'a special religious place' or 'look-out place', neither of which can be suggested here with any confidence.

There are many 'new farmstead' place-names found throughout the land. However they usually have a clearer modern form than that of **Naunton**, but this is by no means unique. Another place of obvious beginnings is **Sandford**. This stands on the road from Worcester to Gloucester, which crosses a small tributary of the Severn here.

Sheriffs Lench

This is seen as *Lench Alnod* in 716, and *Scherreuelenche* in 1221 (*see* Ab Lench). The addition here to differentiate from other like-named settlements refers to this being the home of the sheriff of the district.

Shell

Found in 956 as *Scylfweg* and as *Scelves* in Domesday, the origins here are identical with that of Selly Oak – Old English *scylf* is '(place at) the bank, slope or ledge'.

Shelsey Beauchamp and Walsh

Early records of these places include *Sceldeslaeghe*, *Celdeslai*, *Caldeslei*, and *Sceldeslega* from the eleventh century, the additions appearing by the mid-thirteenth century as *Scheldeslegh Beauchampe* and *Seldesleg le Waleis*.

The two places are opposite each other on the banks of the River Teme, and have the common element derived from '(place at) Sceld's woodland clearing'.

The Beauchamps held their manor from the twelfth century, while by 1212 Johannes Walensis (whose name means 'Welsh') had taken the helm at Shelsey Walsh.

One of the most popular animals featured in pub names is the lion. Usually found with a defining colour, this is clearly a heraldic reference as found with **The Lion Inn**.

Shoulton

There is some doubt as to the origins of the first element here. It may be something akin to Saxon *sceolege*, 'squinting', which would have been used as a nickname. However the second element-*tun*, 'farmstead', could be preceded by an alternative name for **Lawern Brook**, which does meander along all of its course.

Shrawley

This place is listed as *Escreueleia* in 1150, and *Schraveleg* in 1212, but it is the record dated 804 as *Scraefleh* which tells of the derivation. Saxon *scraef-leah* is '(place at) the woodland glade by a scraef'.

Old stone signpost near Shrawley.

The element *scraef* is found quite often in English place-names, yet rarely is the original reference understood for it can have several meanings. In the singular it is used to mean 'cave, den, or hovel', the plural form is identical and used in the sense 'hollow, ravine, etc'. There is a recess in a hill not far from here which may well be what the element refers to, although this will never be certain.

Incidentally, the **New Inn** at Shrawley has not been 'new' since the middle of the seventeenth century. Indeed, such is the antiquity of the place that it is unknown if it was 'new' in the sense of there being an inn already in Shrawley when this place was built (as is the case with the majority of pubs named thus), or if this refers to the 'new' premises of the innkeeper.

Sodington Hall

None could have predicted that a place-name of such simple beginnings would have evolved into something such as this. (We would expect to find the complex original to have become simplified over the centuries.)

Found as *Suthintuna gemaeru* in 957 and *Sudtone* in Domesday, the name comes from Old English *suth in tune* – literally 'south in the village' or 'the southern end of the settlement'. The record of *Suthintuna* is actually a folk-name derived from this for 'the dwellers south in the village' (a Saxon version of EastEnders, so to speak).

Spetchley

Old English *spec-leah* is seen in records such as *Spaeclea* in 967 and *Speclea* in Domesday. This tells us this place was 'the woodland clearing where meetings were held'.

From the late sixteenth century the Berkeley family held lands in the region for 400 years. The sign at the **Berkeley Arms** shows the family crest.

Stanford on Teme

There can be no doubt this comes from a river crossing here as 'the stony ford'. The stones could well have been placed there in order to provide a firm base to prevent the wheels of carts from sinking into the muddy river bed, in which case one would presume the crossing would have required constant maintenance and thus travellers would have been liable to pay a toll fee of some description.

Early forms include *Stanfordesbrycg* in 1030, *Stanford* in 1086, and *Stanford on Temede* in 1317 (for the river-name, *see* Teme).

Staunton

This is another 'stony' name as with Stanford. Here the record of *Stantun* in 972 points to 'the farmstead on stony ground'. Sometimes this name is also used to refer to a prominent stone or stones (used as a landmark, or boundary marker), and although the early forms suggest otherwise, it seems unlikely that the community would settle for farmland with plenty of stones when there were so many alternatives available.

Stildon

Listed as *Stilladun, Stilledune* and *Stillindon,* this seems to have originated from Saxon *stiell,* which is often used to refer to 'a place for catching fish'. As the usual method was to apply a can or wickerwork trap to snare the fish, we can assume this came from a word 'trap'. As this place is on a hill (Saxon *dun*) it is logical to assume this is 'the hill where traps for animals were placed'.

Stock and Bradley

Records of this place begin with *Stokke and Bradeleye* in 1376, and *Stoke Bradley* in 1418. Stock is probably Old English *stocc,* meaning 'stock' or 'stockade', rather than *stoc* as would be suggested by the early fifteenth-century record (*see* Severn Stoke). Bradley is undoubtedly '(place at) the broad woodland glade'. It is clear we are talking of what were originally two places, so close they became indistinguishable after expansion.

Stockton on Teme

Early forms of this name as *Stoctun* in 957 and *Stotune* in Domesday do not help us to see if this is Old English *stoc-tun,* 'farmstead with or belonging to a stoc ('special place' – *see* Severn Stoke)'; or if this is *stocc-tun,* 'stockaded homestead (literally 'of logs')', although the latter seems unlikely.

The addition refers to its location on the River Teme, which is explained in detail under that entry.

Stoke Bliss

The common element of Stoke is covered at length under Severn Stoke. The addition here is first seen in the thirteenth century as *Stoke de Blez.* Bliss is the family name de Blez or Bledis which apparently refers to the town of Blay in Normandy.

Stoke Prior

Lying just south of Bromsgrove, and home to the Avonscroft Museum of Buildings, Stoke Prior's first element is discussed under Severn Stoke. The additional 'prior' is to differentiate from other stokes (the most common English place-name by far) and refers to it being held by Worcester church.

Local place-names include **Sharpway Gate**. Two roads meet here at a sharp angle forming a 'point', hence the name. The additional 'Gate' was added much later, and can hardly be Saxon *geat*, 'pass, gap', but probably came from a gated field near the road junction. The name of **Hen Brook** is not a reference to poultry: hen is used here to indicate waterfowl, particularly the moorhen.

Stone

Domesday's eleventh-century record of *Stanes* tells us the Saxon beginnings are either *stan* or *stanas*, 'the stone or stones'. Just what the name refers to is unclear, but we can assume it must have been significant to those who lived here, in which case the 'stones' could well be boundary markers if plural, or the site of some religious rite, Christian or otherwise, if singular. Several places still commemorate the ancient ceremony of 'beating the boundary': in early spring the community tour the boundary to bless the town or village in the hope of warding off evil and/or an excellent harvest.

Stoulton

This name is derived from the Saxon *stol-tun*, which is exactly how it appears in the record of 840. 'The farmstead or village with seat' refers to this place being the meeting place for this hundred, an administrative sub-division of the county.

Stour, River

This is a British river-name listed as *Stur* in 686, *Sture* in 866, and *Stoure* in 1300. The origins are identical with that of the Stura in Italy (recorded as Stura by Pliny). It derives from the root *steu*, related to Sanskrit *sthavard*, meaning 'firm', and Latin *stauro* and Old Norse *staurr*, meaning 'a pole'. Thus the river-name here means 'strong, powerful one', referring to the current (*see also* Teme, River).

Stourbridge

Now considered a part of the West Midlands, the name is comparatively recent, first seen in 1255 as *Sturburg*. It clearly refers to a 'bridge over the River Stour', and would probably have referred to a footbridge.

A settlement had existed here well before that recorded in the thirteenth century, and well before any 'bridge' here. However, as no surviving record has ever been found of any earlier name, we will probably never know what Stourbridge was known as in earlier times.

The prosperity of the town is based on the manufacture of glass, which began (as did many of England's industries) with the arrival of Huguenot refugees in the sixteenth century. It reached a peak in the nineteenth century, local clay proving a valuable and readily available resource.

The name of **Prescott** indicates this area was once 'the cottage(s) of the priests', not used by the men of the cloth, but situated on land held by the church. The name is normally found as 'Preston'.

Stourport-on-Severn

This place-name is not found earlier than 1775 as Stourport, while the somewhat obvious origin is 'port at the confluence of the rivers Stour and Severn'. Certainly there was a settlement here prior to the eighteenth century, although just what this place was called before Domesday is a mystery.

If the Saxon name included the element 'port' it may not have been used in the modern sense, for the Anglo-Saxons also used the same word for 'town, market town, market, and gate'. **Larford** is on the Severn a mile downstream from Stourport. A charter of 706 grants the use of a weir here for catching fish and remains of the weir are still apparent. The name has nothing to do with the weir, but comes from Saxon *laefer-ford*, '(place at) the river-crossing where rushes are abundant'.

Possibly the most interesting street-name in the county is that of **Gilgal**; it is found several times as a place-name in Jordan and Israel. A gilgal is a stone circle, the most important being that near Jericho where the Old Testament tells us the twelve tribes camped having entered Palestine. The circle at Stourport is formed by the street itself together with Mitton Street, with the Brindley canal cutting directly through the centre. There is evidence clearly visible from the air of an early Saxon church just to the north of this circle, which would invariably have been built on or near the site of earlier pagan rituals. **Tan Lane** is self-explanatory as the road which led to the tannery that once flourished here.

From the proverb 'a bird in the hand is worth two in the bush', the **Bird In Hand** public house conveys the same message. The **Brindley Arms** on Minster

The upper canal basin at Stourport-on-Severn between the Worcestershire/Staffordshire canal and the River Severn.

The lower locks at Stourport-on-Severn, dropping 50 ft from the canal and the last steps linking the Severn to the Trent.

Road commemorates the work of James Brindley, the engineer who was chiefly responsible for the network of canals across the land that are enjoying a new lease of life today as a leisure attraction. Many 'old' names today are not really old by comparison. The **Old Beams** is traditionally said to have incorporated the beams of the earlier building on the site, although the name is as likely to have been brought by a new landlord from his former establishment.

Strensham

Found in 972 and 1212 as *Strengesho* and *Strengesham* respectively, the two forms are originally 'Strenge's *hoh*' and later 'Strenge's *ham*'. Old English *hoh* was 'a spur of land', while ham here means 'homestead'.

The personal name is derived from the Saxon *strenge* meaning 'strong', and would have been applied originally as a nickname.

Suckley

The only record of note is that of Domesday as *Suchelei*. This is 'the woodland clearing frequented by sparrows', from Old English *succa-leah*.

Suckley was the first place ever to dispense with the hand-picking of hops, for the world's first hop-picking machine was developed, built and tested here.

Locally we find **Bastenhall**, a name which tells us this was once 'the nook of land of a man called Basta'.

Sutton

A common place-name, normally found with a distinguishing addition. Here, however, is 'the southern farmstead' from Saxon *suth-tun*.

T

Tardebigge

Found as *Taerdebicgan* in *c.* 1000 and *Terdeberie* in Domesday, the name is still obscure in origins and meaning despite the early records. Indeed, of all the place-names which have been defined, this is among the very few which have no identifiable origins whatsoever, whereas normally there are at least one or two who are willing to suggest some origins (irrespective of how tenuous the suggested origin may be). Tardebigge is one of the few places to have appeared in three counties: Staffordshire from around 1100 to 1266, when it became a part of Warwickshire until the boundary changes of 1844 finally placed it within Worcestershire.

Tutnall is found as *Tothehel* in Domesday; this appears to be a corruption, for later in 1262 and again in 1275 the name appears as *Tottenhull* which is '(place at) Totta's hill'. An Anglo-Saxon charter of 911 describes a battle between the Angles and the Danes fought at Tootenhall, which was originally thought to refer to Tettenhall in Staffordshire; however, many now believe the open, treeless slopes of Tutnall to have been the true site of the engagement. Further weight is added to this argument by the reference to *Bremesbyrig* in the same charter, where Ethelfleda built a defensive fort. Tutnall has long been the site of human habitation; its open, raised situation provided a readily defendable position, and Neolithic artifacts have been discovered here.

The Sidnals is derived from the Saxon for '(place at) the broad corner of land'. The region known as **Hewell Grange** takes its name from the Old English *ae-wylm*, 'the waterspring'; while **Raglis** is a much-shortened form of the family name recorded here from at least 1275 as de Raggeleye – who almost certainly took their name from Ragley in Warwickshire.

Teddington

Despite the plentiful early forms, this place-name cannot be defined with any degree of certainty. We find *Teottingtun* in 780, *Teotintun* in 964, *Teottincgtun* in 969, and *Teotintune* in Domesday, which together point to 'the farmstead of the family or followers of Teotta'. This personal name is not recorded but is doubtless this or something similar.

Teme, River

This is an Old British or Celtic river-name thought to represent 'the dark one'. Appearing in records since the mid-eighth century as *Temede, Temede Stream* and *Temedan*, it is related to the river-names Tame and Welsh Taff and Taf. Indeed we can also be certain this is akin to Old Irish *temen*, 'dark', and Sanskrit *tamas*, 'darkness'. Some suggest most river-names beginning 'T-' have a source in the Old Celtic *ta*, literally 'to melt' and used in the sense of 'fluid' or 'water'. This may be a very uncertain definition, indeed a highly unsatisfactory one, but it could be a valuable clue to a much more ancient question.

As we have seen throughout this book, river-names are invariably buried way back in time. A reliable water source was clearly a major factor when the agricultural way of life superseded the nomadic existence. Furthermore, the larger rivers would have provided important transport routes for trade purposes between these early settlements. What is particularly interesting is the link with Sanskrit, as seen with Teme. This language only had a written form, and is found predominantly on the Indian sub-continent. It has been known for a long time that the languages indigenous to the Indian sub-continent and to most of Europe (known as the Indo-European group) have origins in a single mother tongue. It is reasonable to assume that a word for water and/or river would have been among the first nouns as humans first developed simple verbal communication skills. Hence it is not unreasonable to suggest that clues to the ancient root word for water/river are scattered throughout Europe among the many similar river-names.

Tenbury Wells

Domesday's *Tamedeberie* is the only historical record available, but this is undoubtedly 'the stronghold on the river Teme' (*see* Teme). The additional 'Wells' refers to the spa here and is a recent addition.

The first part of **Sutton Sturmy** is a common place-name found throughout England, so common it is rarely found alone, as here. This 'southern farmstead' is distinguished by the name of the family who held lands here for many years.

Local place-names exhibit a number of the common factors found in district names which, through predominantly local usage only, are more likely to evolve (sometimes at a quite astonishing pace). **Cinders Wood** may seem easy to define but has no connection with burning whatsoever. The true Saxon origin here is *sunder* meaning 'apart' and the basis for the modern word 'asunder'. Here it is used in the sense of 'away from (the main body of the settlement)'.

Splash Bridge is a corruption which may have been predictable. The real first element here is a word describing a pool, which was crossed in early times by a footbridge. **Terrills Farm** is a personal name, despite the lack of any possessive indicator. Records show this to have been the domain of the Tyrel family by 1275. It is a strange quirk of minor place-names that wherever a personal name is indicated by an apostrophe, invariably the origin is not a personal name. Yet whenever the possessive 's' is either not shown or missing altogether, the origins nearly always show that such should be shown (*see Terrills Farm*).

Throckmorton

Listings as *Throcmortune* and *Trochemeron* show the first element here to be Saxon *throc*. This word was used to describe a supporting piece of wood, or a wooden spar on which another more important piece of equipment relied in order to function. We mainly find this element used to refer to the piece of timber on which the ploughshare was fixed. Here, however, the reference can be taken to mean a trestle support for a jetty, so we can take the name of Throckmorton to have originated as 'lake with a wooden jetty'. There seems little likelihood these were used as landing points for boats; more likely to have been places where the women washed clothes.

Tibberton

As evidenced from the tenth-century record of *Tidbrihtincgtun* and Domesday's *Tidbertun*, this name is derived from 'the farmstead or village of a man called Tidbeorht'.

There is no doubt as to the meaning of **Ravenshill**, but does this refer to the bird or is it a nickname? Of course we will never know the answer for certain, but logically the personal name would be the more likely origin.

Agricultural it was, and so the region remains. Hence it is no surprise to find this reflected in the name of a local pub. An old saying of 'God speed the plough', where 'speed' was used to wish for success, lends its name to the **Speed the Plough**. This establishment is in **Plough Road**, which would have predated the pub by many years.

Trimpley

Another Saxon personal name, this time suffixed by *leah*. Listed in Domesday as *Trinpelei* and belonging to the king, this is '(place at) the woodland clearing of a man called Trympa'.

Tutnall

Saxon *hyll* is seen here together with a personal name giving '(place at) the hill of a man called Totta'. The only records of this are as *Tothehel* in Domesday and in 1262 as *Tottenhull*.

U

Upton upon Severn

An obvious origin, seen only as *Uptune* and *Uptun* in the ninth and eleventh centuries respectively, this is 'the higher farmstead on the River Severn (for discussion of the river-name, *see* Severn).

Upton's history is so tied to the river, it is somewhat surprising to find no mention of it in Domesday. Certainly the river would have been the main highway

This bell tower (known as the Pepperpot) is all that remains of the old church of St Peter and St Paul in Upton on Severn. It is the oldest building in the town.

for transporting timber, salt, wine, cider, etc. Later years saw the trow, a two-masted sailing vessel, the major mode of transport. The tide conveyed these craft as far as Gloucester and, when the wind failed, they were hauled great distances by the bow halliers (no mean task when the river was in spate). These men were probably responsible for the town's reputation of rowdiness. Court records abound with tales, including Scots Greys being summoned from Worcester in 1832 to disperse the men who were rioting in protest at horses being used along the towpath. There are also numerous references to river pirates, and narratives of men from Upton casting such gigantic nets that all the salmon were caught, creating uproar from those awaiting the bounty of the annual migration upstream.

As the inland port reached its peak, so did tales of squalor. Laws were passed to prevent butchers from emptying cows' bellies into the streets; and to ensure that no dungheap was allowed to stand for a period of more than sixteen days! With pigsties on the bridge to further compound the problem, it is not surprising that recurring plagues swept through the town for many years. Eventually the coming of the railway saw an end to Upton's importance as an inland port. The great floods of 1852 demolishing the old bridge was seen as the signal that what had been was gone, and would be no more.

Local place-names here include **Tiltridge Farm**, the modern form a somewhat corrupted version of the original Saxon which literally meant 'habitats on a slope', used here to suggest 'residences' from which we can be fairly certain there were a number of different forms of living accommodation ranging from huts to comparatively substantial houses.

The **Drum and Monkey** public house remembers the travelling showmen who toured the land accompanied by a monkey who performed tricks on a drum. One of the most unusual pub names in the county is that of **The Gay Dog Inn**. It is likely to have been transplanted from a pub at Lower Quinton in Stratford-on-Avon, and hence has the same origins. Here a former owner, Joe Braddon, was famous for his prize-winning boxer dogs and went on to become a well-respected judge at the Crufts Dog Show.

From the time when travellers were always on the look-out for a place of refreshment, for both them and their horses, comes the name of the **Horse and Groom**.

W

Wadborough

With records such as *Wadbeorgas* in 972 and *Wadberge* in 1086, this name is derived from Saxon *wad-beorg*, 'the hill where woad grows'.

Trades are often featured in pub names, originally representing the former craft of an early innkeeper, or even used as an invitation to entice workers within that trade to assemble within. The **Masons Arms** is found throughout the land, always depicting the crest of the trade somewhere on the sign.

Wannerton

Domesday's *Wenuertun* and *Wenfertone* in 1275 show this *tun* or 'farmstead' is derived from the old name of the stream here. The ninth-century record of *Wenfero* is just another of the river-names where the etymology has remained obscure.

Warley Salop and Wigorn

The name that both these places derive from is Saxon *weorf-leah*, as evidenced by records such as *Werweleie*, *Weruesleg*, *Worveleg* and *Weruele*. Hence these places were 'farmstead renowned for its cattle pasture', which presumably meant an excellent supply of dairy products.

The distinguishing affixes of these two places reveal that while Warley Wigorn was always a part of Worcestershire, Warley Salop once fell within the borders of neighbouring Shropshire.

Warndon

The eleventh-century records of *Wermedun* and *Warmendone* could have one of two meanings. This is either '(place at) Waerma's hill' or possibly 'the people of Waerma's place by the hill'.

The name of the **Gleden Brook** is of Saxon origin meaning 'the brook where reeds flourish'. It seems unlikely that this is the original name; we would expect an earlier British name but no records of such have survived. **Tollerdine** is an interesting place-name, which literally means 'toll estate'. The thing about place-names, indeed any proper noun, is that they indicate something notable about a particular item, person or place wherever possible. It is unlikely that a name would refer to a toll as this would have been normal practice at the time, and thus we can reasonably assume, even without written documentation, that the name refers to a region which was toll-free.

A rarely used phrase today, the **Poacher's Pocket** was a large pocket on the inside of a long coat, used to conceal ill-gotten gains from the eyes of the gamekeeper without closer examination. Just why such a name would be adopted by a public house is difficult to understand, unless it was intended to convey the suggestion of plenty of room and/or privacy.

Welland

Seen as *Wenelande* in 1189 and *Weneland* fifty years later, the first element is thought to be a stream-name Wen from Welsh *gwyn* (feminine form *gwen*) meaning 'white'. The place is on a stream which joins **Wynd Brook** (recorded as *Wenbroc* in 963). If both arms were once known as Wem, then this place was at the land between.

The region once used to graze animals, now known as **Assarts Common**, has a first element which comes from Old French. This word *assart* is still used today by the legal profession, specifically to describe an area designated for building or farming, where previously the land had either been forested or deemed to be 'wasteland'.

Westmancote

The earliest forms are little different from the modern version as *Westmonecote* and *Westmancota*. It is easy to see this as 'the cottages of the western men', which must surely refer to the homes of Welshmen.

Westwood Park

Early listings as *aet Westwuda* in 972 and *Westwod* in 1206 are not necessary to see this is '(place at) the western wood'.

White Ladies Aston

As with Aston Fields, early records of *Eastun* in 977 and *Estun* in Domesday shows this was originally an outlying 'eastern settlement' of a larger place. Such common names often appear with a second element to prevent confusion. The earliest record of the longer version of the name dates from 1481 as *Whitladyaston*, which refers to the manor being held by the Cistercian nuns of Whitstones.

Whittington

It seems almost every other county has a Whittington somewhere. However, they do not have the same meaning. Records of Whittington in Worcestershire include *Huuitington* in 816 and *Hwitintun* in 989, which still do not clarify the origin. This could be either 'the farmstead of the family or followers of Hwita', or simply just 'Hwita's farmstead', or if this is not a personal name it could even be 'the white farmstead'.

Wichenford

Thirteenth-century records of *Wiceneford* and *Wicheneford* show this to be 'ford at or near the wych elm trees'.

Locally we find **Rugg's Place**, which has no connection with rugs or a personal name. This place-name is derived from the Saxon meaning '(place at) the ridge'. Also near here is **Colkett's Farm**, which like many other place-names displaying a possessive 's' that erroneously suggests a personal name. In fact the origin here is Old English meaning 'cold or exposed cottages'.

Wick

The only ancient listing is in Domesday as *Wiche*, the Saxon word *wic*, used to represent 'the dwelling, a specialised farm, dairy farm, or trading settlement'. **Lower Wick** is of similar derivation, with a clear distinguishing addition.

The **Maple Leaf** is a pub at Lower Wick which reflects the names of the roads constructed here in the 1960s, all named after places in Canada.

Wick Episcopi

The same definition is here as for Wick, although *Wican* in 757, *aet Wican* in 961, *Bisshopeswick* in 1221, and *Wyk Episcopi* in 1291 offer no clues to the sense in which Saxon *wic* is used here. What is certain is the origin of the addition, which refers to ownership by the Bishop of Worcester.

Wickhamford

Recorded as *Wicwona* in 709, *Wiquene* in 1086, and *Wikewaneford* in 1221, this has similar origins to Childswickham. Here it is 'the ford at the place called Wicwon'. The name of *Wicwon* is possibly related to Old Welsh *guic*, 'lodge, wood' and *guoun*, 'plain, meadow, or moor', although this is by no means certain.

There are innumerable examples of English place-names being transferred to the United States of America, probably appearing in more than one state. However easy it is to see why this happened, examples of American place-names being transferred back to England are very rare. Yet there is one at Wickhamford in **Bunkers Hill**. There are no records of this name prior to the date of the Battle of Bunker Hill in 1775, one of the few victories for the British to celebrate during the American War of Independence, so there is no reason to suppose the name ever existed prior to this. It seems logical to assume that whomsoever held the land here around this time had some connections with those who fought in this British military success (probably the family of one of the British officers, or at the very least a soldier). In complete contrast, the arms of the family of George Washington are displayed in the local church here.

Another local place-name is that of **Press Meadow**, which is derived from the Old English meaning 'priest's meadow', a reference to it being held by the church.

Wilden

The village of Wilden is found in the twelfth century as *Wineladuna* and *Winelduna*, and as *Wiveldon* a century later. The latest record can be discounted as erroneous and thus this name is derived from 'Winela's hill' from the Saxon *dun*. This personal name is a side-form of Winel, and possibly started as a nickname.

Witley, Great and Little

These two places have many early records, including *Wittlaeg* in 964, *Witleah* in 969, *Wihtlega* in the eleventh century, *Witlege* in Domesday, and *Whitele Major* in

Witley Court, prior to the devastating fire in the early nineteenth century, was one of the most splendid homes in England (and certainly the most expensive to build).

1275. The first element is Old English *wiht* meaning 'to bend, curve, yield' making this 'the woodland clearing by the bend'. The 'bend' in question is a deep recess in Abberley Hill at Great Whitley.

Wolverley

Derived from a Saxon personal name and Old English *inga*-leah, this name has early records as *Wulfferdinleh* from 866, and *Ulwardelei* in Domesday; this is '(place at) the woodland clearing of the family or followers of a man called Wulfweard'. Wolverley Court was the birthplace of the printer John Baskerville (1706–75).

A region near Wolverley is **Aust Cliff**, which gave its name to farms in the area. This is derived from the Saxon 'Ealhstan's cliff', although the Saxon meaning of 'cliff' could mean anything from a steep slope – probably used here to refer to the settlement located at the base of the slope, as it seems improbable to have attempted to build on the slope itself.

In Saxon times the settlement which was known as 'Aecci's place', is seen today in names such as **Axborough Farm**, **Axborough Wood**, and **Axborough Lane**. The same Old English tongue is also seen in 'the wet valley', which is known today as **Solcum Farm**.

Often portrayed with a humorous sign, the **Live and Let Live** is a pub name which appeared in the nineteenth century. The owner or landlord of the time would have used the name as his personal and very public comment on a situation he considered to be unfair. Just what was being protested about here is unknown, for the incident was usually long forgotten many years before the memory of the protestor. The **Lock Inn** is another where the association with the canal is used as a play on words to offer an invitation to step within – albeit a somewhat tongue-in-cheek one.

Wolverton

There can be no doubt of the personal name here. Records such as *Wulfringctun* in 977, *Wulfringtun* in 984, and in Domesday as *Ulfrintun* show Wolverton to be from 'the farmstead of the family or followers of Wulfhere'.

Worcester

Early records are plentiful, including *Weogorna civitas* in 691, *Wigranceastre* in 717, and *Wirecestre* in 1086. Saxon *caester* refers to a former Roman stronghold, hence this is 'the Roman town of the Weogora tribe'. The Weogora were a tribe who probably took their name from an Old British or Celtic name meaning 'winding river', an excellent description of the Severn around which they lived,

Worcester Cathedral, as seen from the river.

although their area was large and the name is not necessarily taken from the River Severn.

The name for the Roman fort at Worcester is thought to have been *Vertis*, which again seems to have a sense of 'winding', and may well have been a Latinised version of a Celtic root which was itself related to Latin *vertere*, meaning 'to turn'. The cathedral has a Norman chapter house and an eleventh-century crypt, rebuilt by Bishop Wulfstan in about 1080. The tomb of the much-maligned King John lies here.

There is still only one bridge over the river (the other is for rail traffic only); built in 1771, it was widened in 1931. Meticulous planning over the years has resulted in less traffic congestion leading to the bridge, despite the greatly increased volumes of traffic. Restoration of the cathedral was completed in 1874, with the result close to how it looked in the thirteenth century.

Street-names around Worcester, as with most places, commemorate local families and dignitaries linked to the city. **Dent Close** recalls John Dent (1757–1855), a glover who became mayor in 1825 and high alderman in 1826. In 1837 he retired from public life and moved from his home in the city, purchasing Sudeley Castle in Gloucestershire, the last resting place of Catherine Parr, sixth wife of Henry VIII.

There is surely no place in England where so many swans gather in one place as along the Kneve in Worcester.

William Stallard started a wine business in 1808. His son Josiah later took over the company while his eldest son (also called William) became a leading figure in local politics for many years. The family gave their name to **Stallard Road**.

Pierpoint Street recalls Matthew Pierpoint FRCSE, who was appointed as a surgeon at the Worcester Infirmary in October 1819. Another medical man gave his name to **Hebb Street**. Christopher Henry Hebb (1794–1861) was a member of the Royal College of Surgeons who also spent time as a city councillor.

Former alderman, sheriff, and mayor Richard Padmore is commemorated by **Padmore Street**. Following a successful career in local politics, he was elected to represent the city in the House of Commons in 1789. **Carden Street** recalls the life of Thomas Carden. Born in 1738, he had a successful clothing business and also spent time as a councillor. When he died in 1836 he was buried in St Nicholas church.

While **Rowley Hill Street** would seem to take its name from a place-name, it was actually named in honour of Thomas Rowley Hill (although the family names were clearly taken from place-names). Born in 1816, he ran a company which manufactured vinegar and he also served as sheriff and as mayor of the city.

Another local businessman, George Williamson (1845–1918), is marked by **Providence Street**. The Williamson family business was a major employer during the latter half of the nineteenth century, their sealed metal cigarette tins being exported to all four corners of the globe. The street is named after the factory where the world-famous tins were produced, the Providence Works. **Sherriff Street** does not mark the ancient office, or indeed anyone who held the same. The spelling shows this came from a former councillor and mayor, Alexander Clunes Sherriff (1816–78). While the office did not provide the name of the street, it is the origin of the family name, although the sheriff of where is unknown.

Wood Terrace recalls the life of Mrs Henry Wood. Daughter of Thomas Price, she inherited control of the glove factory but is best known as a novelist. A prolific writer, *East Lynne, Mrs Halliburton's Troubles, The Channings, The Shadow of Ashlydyat* and *Rowland Yorke* are just a few of her works. She died in 1887 at the age of seventy-three and is buried alongside other famous individuals in Highgate Cemetery, London.

Laslett Street is named after William Laslett (1801–84). After a career as a solicitor and a barrister, he was elected to the House of Commons. However, he will be best remembered for founding the almshouses in Friar Street.

George William Lyttleton (1817–76), the fourth baron Lyttleton, became Lord Lieutenant of Worcester and was responsible for colonial affairs under Sir Robert Peel's government. He is particularly associated with New Zealand, where Port Lyttleton was named in his honour, and **Lyttleton Street** in Worcester.

Lavender Road takes its name from John Pearkes Lavender (1772–1861). A whitesmith, with premises on the corner of the Shambles and Church Street, he served the city as a councillor, sheriff and mayor.

Lechmere Crescent is named from a family long associated with Worcestershire, first gaining lands in the county under William the Conqueror. Several members of this family from the Low Countries have left their mark on history, among them Judge Lechmere who was a well-known figure during the reign of Charles I and under Cromwell's leadership; Sir Anthony Lechmere, who made his mark on Worcester as a partner of the Old Bank; and during the nineteenth century from 1876 Sir Edmund Lechmere rose to prominence as a member of parliament.

Another family provided the name of **Sandys Road**. Edwin Sandys was Bishop of Worcester from 1559, taking over as Bishop of London in 1570; Sir Samuel Sandys is recorded as taking residence at Ombersley Manor from 1614; and another Samuel Sandys held the offices of Speaker of the House of Lords and First Lord of Trade from 1761.

William Hamilton, the second to hold such a title, is remembered by **Hamilton Road**. He died from injuries received fighting for the Royalists at the Battle of Worcester.

Henry Wakeman (1799–1858) held land in the county and is noted to have been an extremely likeable and easy-going man, who seemed more intent on ensuring his tenants were able to live a life of comparative comfort than lining his own pockets to excess. He later served as a magistrate and his life is commemorated by **Wakeman Street**.

Nash's Passage recalls two members of that family: John Nash (1590–1662), a clothier who served as sheriff, mayor and was elected to the Houses of Parliament during the reign of Charles I; and Dr Nash, whose two volumes of *The History of Worcestershire* are still a valuable source of information today.

The Vernon family are known to have been active in the county by 1580. Sir Harry Vernon held office as justice of the peace, high sheriff, and deputy lieutenant. Together with his wife Lady Georgina, they were instrumental in setting up what became known as the County Nursing Association. Their efforts are commemorated by **Vernon Park Road** and **Georgina Avenue**.

John, Lord Somers, had his seat at Clifton Stoke and commanded a troop of Cromwell's army during the Civil War. His sons and their sons served as chancellor, solicitor-general and other high political offices. The family's efforts are worthy of the naming of **Somers Road**.

Wylds Lane is taken from the name of a family of clothiers, who were active in Worcestershire for many years from the sixteenth century.

The Shambles was a common name for any street where shops and/or market stalls dominated. This ancient thoroughfare was the stronghold of bakers until the sixteenth century; thereafter records of indiscretions by tradesmen show that butchers had largely replaced them. Although the majority of medieval town streets are narrow in comparison to today, all streets known by this name are noticeably narrow and historically have high buildings on either side. That these show such similarities is no coincidence. In the days before refrigeration, when upper storeys of buildings would overhang, blocking the sunlight was the best method of keeping produce cool and thus fresh.

The Butts was so named after a royal command, issued on 3 May 1549 by Edward VI, ordered that butts be placed at the city's gates. This has nothing to do with what may be suggested in modern terminology, referring to a defensive position. From the Old French *butte*, this could refer to a target for archery, the wall or mound of earth erected behind the target to prevent stray arrows finding alternative targets, or (as is the case here) artificial walls or mounds to protect the archers and still allow them to fire upon the enemy.

Two miles to the north-west of Worcester is **Atchen Hill**, recorded as *Aerinc weg* in 963 and *Aettinge gaerstun* in 970. The Saxon elements *weg* and *gaerstun* mean 'way' and 'meadow' respectively. This probably means that the hill took its modern name from the pathway, the meadow, and the settlement which grew up here. No early record of the hill-name survives, but it seems unlikely to have been

Worcester's German twin town is mentioned on this modern city sign.

'the hill of the family or followers of Aetti'. Another hill-name is that of **Mucken Hill** 4 miles south-east of Worcester. Recorded as *Mucenhill* in Domesday and *Mokenhulle* two centuries later, this is '(the place at) Muca's hill'.

The village of **Barbourn** is named after the brook, recorded as *Beferburn*, which ran into the Severn. This must be a very ancient name for this is 'the brook where beavers are seen' and these animals were extinct in England long before the Norman Conquest. Today the brook appears on maps as **Beverbourn**. Two miles further upstream is an area known as **Bevere**, which is from the Saxon for 'beaver island' and refers to a small island in the river here. **Sudbury** is another Saxon name, here 'the southern fortified place'.

With the Welsh border not far away, and in earlier times even closer, it is no surprise to find influences of the Welsh language in Worcestershire (even more widespread in the place-names of Herefordshire and Shropshire). **Cruckbarrow Hill** and **Cruckbarrow Farm** have two elements, the first Old Welsh *cruc* followed by Middle English *berewe*. Both of these words have the same meaning: 'mound, tumulus, or hill'; there is no reason to believe otherwise, for it is common to find hill-names containing the same word from differing languages (as the Saxons had no idea what Old Welsh 'cruc' meant). Hence Cruckbarrow Hill actually means 'hill hill hill'.

Named after a battle of the Crimean War in 1854, the **Alma Inn** refers to the first victory by the Allies over the Russians and takes its name from the river at the scene. In the latter half of the nineteenth century, soldiers who fought here named their daughters Alma, the first time this had been used as a personal name. The Berkeley family have held lands in the county up to the present day; their family crest is displayed on the sign of the **Berkeley Arms**. The **Brunswick Arms** represents the Duke of Brunswick who was killed fighting on the side of the British at Waterloo, and who lived in England for many years.

At Lower Broadheath is the **Dew Drop Inn** – a popular pun found in pub names to invite potential customers to 'do drop in'. Worth noting, although probably entirely coincidental, the motto of the Distiller's Company is 'My speech shall distil as the dew', taken from the Song of Moses in Deuteronomy 32.

A poem by Sir Henry Newbolt in honour of Sir Francis Drake gave rise to **The Drake's Drum** in Worcester. The relevant lines are:

> Take my drum to England, hang et by the shore.
> Strike et when your powder's running low.
> If the Dons sight Devon, I'll quit the port o' Heaven,
> An' drum them up the Channel as we drummed them long ago.

The **Grosvenor Arms** features the crest of that family, the dukes of Westminster, who have held land in Worcestershire and surrounding counties for many years. In the days when a sign was vital to communicate to prospective customers what lay within, a sign such as that outside the **Horn and Trumpet** would indicate a maker and repairer of musical instruments. The public house of today stands on or near the site of the craftsman's premises.

Put two otherwise unrelated nouns together separated by 'and', and with the definite article in front, and you have a name which can only be a public house, the **Lamb and Flag** being an excellent example. Once again this is a heraldic sign, which was used by the Knights Templar, the Merchant Tailor's Company, St John's College, Oxford, and a number of others. Whether these premises refer to any of these, or was taken as the archetypal pub name is uncertain.

Local references are another feature of pub names. Landmarks, people, trades and events are seen in abundance, usually easy to spot as they rarely occur elsewhere. One such example is **The Little Sauce Factory**, derived from the world famous Worcestershire Sauce made by Lea and Perrins who were chemists in Worcester. Similarly the voyage of the Pilgrim Fathers in 1620 is marked by **The Mayflower**, although just how relevant this is to Worcestershire is obscure.

To the Greeks and Romans a Saracen lived a nomadic existence around the area of the Arabian Desert. Later the word came to mean 'Arab' and thus 'Moslem', the latter particularly associated with the Crusades to the Holy Land. Noble families who had fought the Christian cause would often add this to their coat of arms, which was later to be seen on a sign providing the name of a public house on their lands called the **Saracen's Head**.

After many years of use names of pubs are instantly recognisable as such, even if the premises themselves are unknown. Examples include **Lamb and Flag**, **Dog and Ferret**, and **Pig and Whistle**. In recent years this trend has been revived, taking advantage of the opportunity to show a sense of humour and even an advertisement (ironic considering that was the beginnings of the sign and thereafter the names of the establishments). The **Slug and Jug** not only rhymes (making it easy to remember) and is mildly amusing, but also tells us we can consume a 'slug' (measure of spirits) or a 'jug' (a foaming tankard of ale).

For those not conversant with the age-old tradition of swan-upping, then the pub bearing the name of **Swan With Two Nicks** must seem rather odd. This is not a unique name for a pub, indeed the expected variation of 'Two Necks' is actually as common. We know this subject was raised at a meeting of the Antiquarian Society in 1810 by the eminent botanist and explorer Sir Joseph Banks, who will always be remembered for his work while on board the *Endeavour* on its circumnavigation of the globe under the command of Captain James Cook. For many years the **Black Swan** had been used as a pub name, in the mistaken belief that all swans were predominantly white. Having discovered that Australia had a black swan, Sir Joseph returned to these shores and eventually turned his attention to the 'swan with two necks', a pub name which appeared several times in London. Clearly such a creature could not exist (although it made a much better subject for those designing pub signs!) and two necks was an error, albeit at times a deliberate one. The name of the pub refers to the ownership of swans, for centuries limited to royalty until Elizabeth I granted the same privilege to the Dyer's Company and the Worshipful Company of Vintners. The Vintners not only had the obvious connection with taverns the length and breadth of the land, but also marked their ownership of an individual swan with two nicks on the upper mandible.

Worcestershire

The county of Worcestershire is first referred to in the eleventh century as *Wireceastrescir*. The affix is Old English *scir* meaning 'district'.

Wribbenhall

From Saxon *halh* this place is 'the nook of land of a man called Wrybba'. Early listings of this name include *Gurberhale* in 1086 and *Wrubbenhale* in 1160.

Wychbold

Listed as *Uuicbold* in 692, and *Wicelbold* in 1086, this place-name is derived from the Old English *wic-bold*, 'dwelling near the trading settlement'.

Wyre Forest

Hill, river, and indeed forest-names are often shrouded in antiquity. As comparatively permanent landmarks such places were known, and thus named, from the earliest times of human habitation. Furthermore, these permanent features have a tendency to retain the earliest names, yet are corrupted over the centuries as the language evolves from the earliest (unknown) tongues, through Old British, Latin, Saxon, Norman French, Middle English right through to the modern day (where it still continues to change, albeit at a much slower rate today owing to the predominance of the written language and the ability of the vast majority to read and write).

The earliest record of the Wyre Forest is as *Weogorena leage* in 816. This is probably an alternative name as it means 'the forest of the Weogoran', the tribe which gave its name to Worcester. As the forest was here long before the tribe, it must have been known as something else prior to this but no record has survived. Later we find *Wyre* in *c.* 1080, *foresta de Wira* in 1177, and *Werewud* in 1239. Hence it is reasonable to assume the earlier name was also Wyre Forest (or Wood), sharing its name with the river. Up to the early ninth century the Wyre Forest occupied a large region on the western bank of the Severn west and north-west of Worcester, although today it has dwindled to such an extent that the only sizeable remnant remaining stands astride the **Dowles Brook**. The river-name is thought to be a Celtic word meaning 'winding river', and certainly any ancient origins would be as simplistic as are all the names of water courses.